PRAISE FOR
LOVE OUTSI

This book will make you think, make you laugh, make you pray. Jimmy Rollins pushes the envelope in a prophetic way, and he does so in a way that will fill your heart with hope.

MARK BATTERSON, LEAD PASTOR, NATIONAL COMMUNITY CHURCH, *NYT* BESTSELLING AUTHOR, *THE CIRCLE MAKER*

Love Outside the Lines is a deeply profound, chain-breaking, culture-shifting message for such a time as this. Jimmy shares this message of unity passionately, vulnerably, and empathetically. He speaks to the generational, cultural, and societal strongholds that plague humanity and gives us handles to conquer them. We cherish Jimmy's friendship, and we respect and believe in the call to action that is *Love Outside the Lines*.

EARL AND ONEKA MCLELLAN, LEAD PASTORS, SHORELINE CITY CHURCH

Jimmy's voice has been influential in the body of Christ, helping us think, love, and look beyond ourselves. He brings a compelling biblical approach to reconciliation, challenging us to listen deep and become the answer to Jesus' prayer: that we would be one. His stories will make you laugh, cry, and evaluate your own perspective. I am thrilled for my friend to have put into writing what he's been living for decades.

DANIEL FLOYD, SENIOR PASTOR, LIFEPOINT CHURCH

What a much-needed message for the world today. Pastor Jimmy's heart for reconciliation and unity is also my heart and God's heart. The magnitude of the message of love and forgiveness shared in this book can change a generation and can change history for the better, if we let it. Don't skip this read just because it may get uncomfortable or difficult. Lean in and listen to what God wants to teach you through this. The hard things are worth it.

TRAVIS GREENE, RECORDING ARTIST, PASTOR
OF FORWARD CITY CHURCH

Jimmy has a God-given gift to build bridges in a world full of barriers. His story, wisdom, and insight are needed now more than ever. *Love Outside the Lines* is packed full of heart-moving, practical stories that will inspire us and teach us how to fight for unity, listen, learn, love, forgive, and celebrate our differences!

SHAWN JOHNSON, SENIOR PASTOR, RED ROCKS CHURCH

Jimmy truly practices what he preaches. *Love Outside the Lines* focuses on reconciliation, fighting for unity while celebrating diversity, and having brutally honest conversations that bring us together instead of tearing us apart. These are aspects of the "kingdom culture" that Jimmy lives and practices as a pastor, husband, father, and friend, and it's a message that each one of us needs in today's divided culture. In a world that is so divided, the world needs a church that is united.

DR. J. TODD MULLINS, SENIOR PASTOR, CHRIST FELLOWSHIP CHURCH

Jimmy Rollins has lived the words that he has penned in *Love Outside the Lines*. Through the spectrum of friendships in his life, Jimmy has embodied what it is to put down one's ego in order to build God's church, a living representation of love. Now, through this book, he provides the guide to be able to "go through Samaria, to start having conversations with people who don't look like us, and to wrestle with the parts of us that are resistant to this." I believe this book is going to help us be the church and truly love outside the lines.

STEPHEN CHANDLER, SENIOR PASTOR OF
UNION CHURCH, AUTHOR, SPEAKER

As kids we are prone to color outside the lines because those boundaries seem powerless. As adults we are challenged to love outside of lines because we are confronted with a culture and our very own hearts that harbor stereotypes, biases, and preferences that deter us from Christ's vision of unity and diversity. In his book, *Love Outside the Lines*, Jimmy has done what I've seen him do for the entirety of our close friendship, equip people to love like Jesus did, bringing the conversation about diversity to the most divided atmospheres. If you want a framework to love others on any side of the line you find yourself on, this book is for you. Why? Because this book does not give us tips, it gives us tools.

WAYNE FRANCIS, CO-AUTHOR OF *GOD AND RACE: A GUIDE FOR MOVING BEYOND BLACK FISTS AND WHITE KNUCKLES*

I'm so glad Jimmy Rollins had the courage to write *Love Outside the Lines*. His story and approach to reaching people outside of the safety of our normal social construct resonated with me deeply. If you've followed him for any period of time, you know this is something he doesn't just write about...he lives it! If you're serious about living the way Jesus modeled for us to live, you have to add this book to your reading list!

DR. DHARIUS DANIELS, AUTHOR OF *YOUR PURPOSE IS CALLING*

Jimmy Rollins' dedication, commitment, and passion for mending the gaps that separate individuals are so encouraging. He uses examples from the life of Jesus as well as his own experiences to show how embracing discomfort ultimately leads to healing and reconciliation. This book has helped serve as a catalyst in my own life for difficult conversations and healthy communication.

CHAD VEACH

For a very long time, I've deeply appreciated the open yet loving candor in my relationship with Jimmy. He is a brilliant man and a clear communicator, and he carries a rare combination of deep wisdom, real integrity, and overwhelming compassion for people. I am very thankful that he has taken the time to write *Love Outside the Lines*. I believe everybody needs to read it to help the Body of Christ get better at bringing understanding, healing, and restoration within diversity. And in that delicate dance, he still keeps Jesus at the center of it all.

RICK BEZET, NEW LIFE CHURCH FOUNDING PASTOR,
AUTHOR OF *REAL LOVE AND BE REAL*

LOVE OUTSIDE THE LINES

BEYOND THE BOUNDARIES OF RACE, DIFFERENCE, AND PREFERENCE

JIMMY ROLLINS

W Publishing Group

An Imprint of Thomas Nelson

Published in Nashville, Tennessee, by W Publishing, an imprint of Thomas Nelson.

Thomas Nelson titles may be purchased in bulk for educational, business, fundraising, or sales promotional use. For information, please email SpecialMarkets@ThomasNelson.com.

Unless otherwise noted, Scripture quotations are taken from The Holy Bible, New International Version®, NIV®. Copyright © 1973, 1978, 1984, 2011 by Biblica, Inc.® Used by permission of Zondervan. All rights reserved worldwide. www.Zondervan.com. The "NIV" and "New International Version" are trademarks registered in the United States Patent and Trademark Office by Biblica, Inc.®

Scripture quotations marked CEV are taken from the Contemporary English Version. Copyright © 1991, 1992, 1995 by American Bible Society. Used by permission.

Scripture quotations marked ESV are taken from the ESV® Bible (The Holy Bible, English Standard Version®). Copyright © 2001 by Crossway, a publishing ministry of Good News Publishers. Used by permission. All rights reserved.

Scripture quotations marked KJV are taken from the King James Version. Public domain.

Scripture quotations marked THE MESSAGE are taken from The Message. Copyright © 1993, 2002, 2018 by Eugene H. Peterson. Used by permission of NavPress. All rights reserved. Represented by Tyndale House Publishers a Division of Tyndale House Ministries.

Scripture quotations marked NKJV are taken from the New King James Version®. Copyright © 1982 by Thomas Nelson. Used by permission. All rights reserved.

Scripture quotations marked NLT are taken from the Holy Bible, New Living Translation. © 1996, 2004, 2015 by Tyndale House Foundation. Used by permission of Tyndale House Ministries, Carol Stream, Illinois 60188. All rights reserved.

Scripture quotations marked WEB are taken from the World English Bible™. Public domain.

Any internet addresses, phone numbers, or company or product information printed in this book are offered as a resource and are not intended in any way to be or to imply an endorsement by Thomas Nelson, nor does Thomas Nelson vouch for the existence, content, or services of these sites, phone numbers, companies, or products beyond the life of this book.

ISBN 978-0-7852-9002-5 (audiobook)
ISBN 978-0-7852-9001-8 (eBook)
ISBN 978-0-7852-8981-4 (TP)

Library of Congress Control Number: 2022938383

Printed in the United States of America

23 24 25 26 27 LSC 10 9 8 7 6 5 4 3 2 1

I dedicate this book to James Rollins. Dad, you are my hero and best friend. Since I was young, you've shown me what it means to love outside the lines. Thank you for always having an eye out for the outcast, the ostracized, and the overlooked. Thank you for teaching me how to live sacrificially by always putting the needs of others first. Thank you for being a bridge builder. You were the first one to ride that ten-speed bike out of Wilson Town. You were the first one to desegregate the public school system in Anne Arundel County. You were the first African American man on the board of the church we grew up in. You have persevered, you have endured, and you have blazed a trail for our entire family. The words on these pages are a direct download from the life you live. Although the words were written by my hand, they were founded by the love in your heart. You have never accepted a boundary, limitation, or obstacle as the end but rather as an opportunity for a new beginning. Thank you for running your leg of the race so well. May the words of these pages echo for generations to come as part of your legacy. I love you, Dad!

CONTENTS

FOREWORD

When it comes to relationships, I go to great lengths to cultivate, nurture, and protect mine at all costs. I know first-hand about the stress, the loneliness, and the pain that comes when you do relationships the wrong way, so I'm an advocate for healthy, whole, life-giving marriages, friendships, business part-nerships, and all those other *-ships* that come along in the sea of life. In fact, on August 6, 2017, I stood on stage as the Lead Pastor of Transformation Church in Tulsa, Oklahoma, and started a sermon series called *Relationship Goals*. Since then, my life has never been the same. That series has now surpassed 25 million views on YouTube and was the inspiration for my first book and *New York Times* bestseller, *Relationship Goals: How to Win at Dating, Marriage, and Sex.*

Now I want to be clear: I'm not sharing all of this as a way to boast about myself. I'll be the first to tell you that none of those accomplishments were because of me. As a Tulsa Community College dropout who hated reading and writing, it could *only* be God. I shared all of that to say that relationships are an important part of who and where I am today. So when my friend, Pastor Jimmy Rollins (I think I'm gonna nickname him Jimmy Ro) told me that his new book, *Love Outside the Lines*, was all about building relationships, I couldn't have been more excited. When he went on to tell me that his new book was all about building relationships outside of race, difference, and preference, I couldn't have been prouder.

I'm an 8 on the Enneagram, which means I'm naturally the person who runs toward a challenge with my boxing gloves strapped tight, ready to fight. A good challenge brings me energy and I respect people who can square up and stand ten toes down when disagreements arise and conversations get hard. In this book, my boy Jimmy Ro is in the ring, ready to box with racism, stereotypes, prejudices, and more, and he's pulling no punches. I'm here to cheer him on because at the end of the day, the only way we're going to see progress is if someone addresses the issues head on. And that someone is Jimmy Ro.

In any boxing ring, it can get a little bloody, a little dirty, a little messy, but I can attest to the fact that the best relationships are not the ones that appear to be picture perfect. No. The best relationships are the ones that have stood the test of time and have come out better on the other side of disagreements, misunderstandings, and disappointments. Back in 2006, Timothy S. Lane and Paul David Tripp wrote a book called *Relationships: A Mess Worth Making*. So I've got a question for you: How much *mess* have you made in your relationships? Now when I say "mess," I don't mean anything toxic, limiting, or detrimental. I mean how often are you willing to ask hard questions, engage in uncomfortable conversations, and initiate reconciliation? If you've never had to deal with that kind of "mess," I question whether you're answering the call to build relationships with people who don't look, think, or act like you. Another way to put it is this: I wonder if you're actually fulfilling the Great Commission (Matt. 28:19).

When God gave me the vision for what Transformation Church would become, He told me very clearly that our congregation would be multi-generational and multi-ethnic. Essentially, every Sunday, our church services would look similar to what I imagine Heaven looks like. While that excited me in ways words will never be able to express, what I wasn't prepared for was how much mental and emotional weight came with leading a church full of people who are much older than me, much younger than me, and who come from countries and cultures all over the world. I am always going to be me no matter who is around, but there's another level of awareness I have to walk in now because, with the influence I have been given to steward, anything I do or say could be grounds for offense. Offense has the potential to destroy relationships. Add in a pinch of pride and a sprinkle of self-righteousness and you've got a recipe that could burn up the potential for relational reconciliation.

Love Outside the Lines gives you the tools you need to extinguish the flames of division, disunity, and dissension in your church and your community so you can go on to fulfill the Great Commission. In this book, you'll get to experience some of the hardships Jimmy Ro has encountered as a Black man in America, but you'll also see examples in Scripture for how we, as the body of Christ, are to embrace the discomfort of looking beyond the lines and barriers that divide us to the hope and future of unity on the horizon. I will warn you: it may get a little uncomfortable, your beliefs may be challenged, and you may question whether or not the "mess" of building relationships and making disciples is worth it. Even in those moments, keep going. I'm a firm believer that leaders are readers, so if you've made the commitment to read this book, I champion you for leading the charge to bridge the divides that keep the love of Christ locked up and confined to our personal safe zones instead of it being shared throughout the world to whomever, whenever, wherever, and, however. Be encouraged as you apply the things you learn in this book. It will get messy along the way, but I promise you—for your life, your legacy, and your eternity—it will definitely be worth it.

Let's go!

Michael Todd, #1 *New York Times* bestselling
author, *Relationship Goals* & *Crazy Faith,*
and lead pastor of Transformation Church

INTRODUCTION:

A CRASH COURSE ON THE GREAT COMMISSION

*Comfort causes us to draw lines, but
love carries us outside those lines.*

When I was in college, I had a friend named Tommy Stoudt.
Tommy was a White guy from Lancaster, Pennsylvania, and I'll
never forget the first time I visited his hometown. We were on
our way to dinner, and I was in my car, following him to the
restaurant.

Lancaster was typically not where you would find a Black
man like me. I was driving a "hooked up" 1995 white Acura
Integra that had custom wheels and would turn heads in any
urban community. On the other hand, Lancaster is Amish
country, where the vehicle of choice is horse and buggy. Folks
in this Amish community had chosen a simple life: farming,

dressing plainly, and avoiding electricity. Or at least that's what I had heard. I had never actually had any personal interaction with the Amish. I was just going off the information Tommy told me.

This was my first opportunity to experience the people and culture for myself up close, and I was captivated by their charm and simplicity.

On my way to dinner, I made my way through this very quaint area of town and my physical appetite was overtaken by the distraction of the new experience. I was intrigued by the obvious differences between Amish culture and my own, and it fascinated me how different our lifestyles were.

I felt like a fish out of water.

This Black man was definitely out of his comfort zone.

I was still following Tommy, but I was so engaged in this new experience that I lost track of maintaining a safe driving distance. I was so distracted by what was unfamiliar to me that I failed to notice that Tommy had stopped at a stop sign. By the time I realized it, it was too late. I tried to slam on my brakes, but I slammed into the back of his car. The car that I valued so much was now damaged. The wonder and curiosity that came with the unfamiliar caused an unexpected collision.

As we got out to assess the damage and make sure we were both okay, an Amish family pulled up in their horse and buggy. "Are you guys okay?" the man asked.

"Yes," I replied. "We're okay!"

This family looked very different from me, and they didn't know us, but our differences didn't matter in that moment. They simply stopped to help us. They didn't care about my looks; they cared about my well-being.

For the first time in my life, I was in close proximity with an Amish family whose culture and lifestyle were completely different from anything I had ever experienced. Although our differences were glaring, our potential need for help and their compassion for our well-being brought our worlds together.

When we step out of our comfort zones and enter someone else's world, we discover that we have a lot more in common than we thought.

Looking back at that moment, what seemed like a chance encounter at the time had a much greater purpose for me. I don't believe it was an accident at all. I think God was teaching me a valuable lesson that I've never forgotten: proximity changes things.

A desire for comfort often causes us to draw lines in our lives. Experiencing new places and cultures can be intimidating. It's a lot easier to be around people who look like us, live like us, and think like us. Difference can bring discomfort, so instead, we set up boundaries for ourselves. We only go to certain parts of town, talk to certain types of people, read certain authors, and watch certain news channels. The problem is, these lines that we draw often keep us from experiencing proximity with people from different walks of life.

I discovered that day, through an unlikely series of events, that journeying down unfamiliar roads can lead to a crash course in experiencing the beauty of diversity and bringing together different worlds on one shared road.

When the Amish family set out for that late-afternoon trip, and I ventured down unknown roads trying to make my dinner reservation, neither of us knew that an accidental collision would bring an opportunity for proximity with a person of another culture with whom we otherwise might never have connected.

In that moment I believe I was beginning to sense God pursuing me and purposing my heart to be a part of repairing the damage of division in our country. I was being convicted to learn about other cultures and help address the problems that arise between people due to a lack of proximity to cultures that are different from our own. I was sensing a pull to head down the road of reconciliation, reach out to the unfamiliar, explore uncharted territory relationally with people, and love people no matter how different we are for the purpose of unifying our divided world.

STEPPING OUT

Jesus grew up in a world full of division; a world full of lines that divided people. But during His ministry He stepped over those lines every chance He had. He intentionally went through the towns His disciples wanted to avoid, talked to the outcasts His friends ignored, and ate meals with those whom most people viewed as enemies. Jesus didn't stay within the lines, and His disciples got to witness firsthand how proximity changes things.

This is a book about stepping out and crossing those lines. We are going on a journey together—a journey that will push you out of your comfort zone and into new conversations, and will challenge you to have some new experiences. Because as followers of Christ, each of us is commissioned to follow Jesus on the path reaching the familiar and the unfamiliar, visiting the likely and the least likely, and exploring both the frequently charted wide roads and the often-avoided, uncharted narrow roads.

We are going to journey together down the roads of reconciliation, explore the less-traveled paths toward unity, and purposefully engage in a crash course on living out the love of Christ with consideration, conviction, and compassion. My goal is that this book will serve as a starting point leading us all on a discipleship journey to see like Jesus sees, love like Jesus loves, and explore the areas in our lives and in our hearts that may be roadblocks to racial reconciliation.

My prayer is that as we venture through the intentional places Jesus visited and the people He encountered, you would encounter His love. In order to carry His love outside the lines, we first have to experience it inside our hearts. When God's love changes us internally, we will begin to see external opportunities to carry that love to the world. We will begin to see our own personal roads of reconciliation that God is calling us to.

Because comfort causes us to draw lines.

But love carries us outside those lines.

START WITH PROXIMITY

There is division in our world due to broken systems, failed strategies, and lack of communication. All the division can be overwhelming and feel impossible to fix. And it's why I want to point toward a practical place to start: proximity.

That's how Jesus started. He didn't stay in heaven; He stepped over the line and left everything to be with us and show us how to do the same. As we explore the Gospels together, we'll see that the roads Jesus walked were roads of reconciliation, restoration, and redemption.

Jesus chose proximity and loved outside the lines. He engaged with people of different backgrounds, lifestyles, and regions. His sacrificial journey to the cross gave Him access to diverse people from diverse places. And in that journey, He established His kingdom by bridging gaps, destroying stereotypes, and demolishing divisions.

It's time for us to learn how to do the same.

Before He left, Jesus told His disciples, "Go and make disciples of all nations" (Matthew 28:19). We call this the Great Commission. It is still our charge today: to explore where we have yet to visit, bridge the relational gap of the unfamiliar, and embrace intentional detours. God invites us into proximity with the unexpected to unite a divided world.

I believe that if we are following Jesus, we are destined to have a collision with Him that causes us to engage with and invest in people from various upbringings, cultures, and lifestyles. That day in Lancaster back in 1995 was a quick crash course in my journey into embracing diversity. God had this disciple on a detour to make diversity and unity my destination.

As we begin our journey together, I promise that you will not be judged for where you were previously, you will not be condemned for your current or past mindsets concerning others from different backgrounds, and you will not be labeled for convictions in the past. I encourage you to check in with yourself and embrace what you are feeling about what you have read.

As you journey through the pages of this book, it is my prayer that you feel passionate, confident, and well-equipped to have conversations and bridge gaps with people from diverse communities. Let this be the road map to reroute the conversation of racial reconciliation in our hearts first, as we earn the right to be called disciples by our obedience to follow Jesus.

It's time to learn to love outside the lines!

ONE

VISION IN THE VALLEY

God is not looking for your opinion;
He is looking for your obedience.

Years ago I was riding in a van that broke down in the middle of a unique place—the Great Rift Valley in Kenya.

Our team was on a mission trip, and we were traveling from Nairobi to Nakuru when our van just stopped. We all looked around in disbelief. There we were: bougie Americans stuck in the middle of the Great Rift Valley, in a country most of us were visiting for the first time. The roads didn't have signs telling us where to find the nearest gas station, and there was no GPS to help us navigate our way. We were stuck—in the middle of nowhere with no connection and no direction.

I was uncomfortable with the whole situation. Our lives

were in the hands of our driver, a native man who was very different from us. He did not speak our language well, but he seemed more comfortable with our predicament than I was. As he got out to assess the severity of our situation, some of the others I was traveling with got out of the van and started walking around—everyone except me. I was staying put. I mean, we were in the Great Rift Valley! There were wild animals out there! We were not on familiar soil where we paid to see animals behind metal fences; we were in the middle of the bush where the only thing between us and the animals indigenous to this territory was the thin, dented metal of this beat-up, broken-down van. Looking around, I took a quick assessment of our situation. Of our group I was the biggest, the slowest, and likely the best-looking meal. So I decided the safest place for me was right there in the van.

We ended up being stuck on the side of what I would barely call a road for about three hours. It felt like a lifetime. Always looking for sermon illustrations as a young preacher, I began to reflect on the dilemma and how the situation resembled a challenge I was facing back home in the States with my family.

THE ROLLINS RIFT

I grew up in the church. In fact, I felt like I spent more time in church than I did outside the walls of the church. As far back as I can remember, our family was always in church, and year after year our commitment to the local church became greater and greater. Sparse attendance became regular attendance, and being a part of the congregation at weekend services grew to being at the church whenever the doors were open. Eventually our "church family" become synonymous with the Rollins family and we were all in. We were a part of every aspect of church ministry.

My mom sang on the worship team and traveled regularly with the senior pastor's wife to sing before she preached. Their ministry grew quickly and had national influence with significant impact. My dad, who was a prison warden and very influential in local government, served on the church's leadership team.

As a child, I remember sitting in the back seat of my dad's Ford LTD, drawing against the grain of those blue velvet seats to pass time on the long drives to and from church. I would over-hear conversation after conversation of my parents discussing the church service and how they were affected in significant ways by the message and worship experience. Car ride after car ride, year after year, I heard passion in those countless conversations about how they were impacted by God's presence and loved see-ing God's people grow in their faith.

When I was a teenager and riding as a passenger in my par-ents' car, I heard my mom share something with my dad that would eventually change the trajectory of our entire family's life. She said, "I believe that God has called our family to serve Him in full-time ministry." I had no idea what that meant. I thought, *Aren't we already in church all the time and our family's schedule is already full?*

What did it mean that God was calling our family? What did

the "call of God" mean for me personally as a teenage boy with aspirations to play in the NFL?

Looking back on those days, I had no idea what it meant to be "called by God," but I did know that when I played the drums during worship time, passed out food at the church food pantry, or spent time with my youth pastor watching him passionately "live out his call," as he described it, I felt such significance, purpose, and fulfillment. It was a feeling I began to hunger for.

Over the years that boy became a young man, and my passion grew whenever I was helping people in need through serving the local church. Being witness to my parents living out God's call taught me that being called by God was simply saying yes to sacrificing my life to serve the purposes of my Creator with everything I had in terms of gifts, talents, time, and resources.

It simply meant that God had uniquely designed me for a specific purpose, and I would find various assignments along my life's journey and maturation where I would get to live out that purpose. It was in serving that I was living out my purpose, and this is where I would find significance, favor, and God's unmerited grace to do what He was calling me to do. As the apostle Paul wrote in 2 Corinthians 1:21–22, "It is God who establishes us with you in Christ, and has anointed us, and who has also put his seal on us and given us his Spirit in our hearts as a guarantee" (ESV).

I was called by God, anointed with His grace, and confirmed by His stamp of approval. I could feel His Spirit commissioning me to serve Him, and I decided to answer that call with a resounding yes in every facet of my life.

Fast-forward to my late twenties: I was working in ministry full-time, married to the woman of my dreams, and driving my own kids to my parents' church. My parents were now following God's call to plant a church called Living Waters Worship Center. The call of God on their lives to lead a church was met with some resistance and challenges; however, there was much fruit from their obedience to God to step out in faith. That fruit was reflected in the lives of all the people who came to receive the hope of Jesus Christ through their ministry. The church grew exponentially, and they were serving God's purposes faithfully.

My wife, Irene, and I were helping and serving in every capacity we could. Ministry became a way of life for us. Our ministry was thriving: what started with about one hundred people when we first launched the church in 1995 had grown to over one thousand people in weekly attendance.

To everyone who attended, and for all those who volunteered to help make church happen, this was the greatest church on the planet. We were helping people, training volunteers, and equipping leaders to do the work of ministry (Ephesians 4:12). Every service was jam-packed each week as if Jesus Himself were in the pulpit preaching.

But something was bothering me. Even though the church was thriving, everyone looked like me, thought like me, dressed like me, and even presumably voted like me. Although we had started out as a diverse expression of the community where we lived, the demographic had changed over time so that most members were Black.

That's where the rift began in my own heart. I started to sense a distance forming between where the church was going and where God was calling me.

Yes, we were "having church," and people were finding freedom and experiencing God, but the steady diet of the same menu kept the same faithful customers coming back each Sunday. Although the seats were full, in them sat carbon copies of a great commission that was limited in its reach to only those who fit the parishioner profile.

The rift kept growing larger and larger.

To many this was what success in ministry looked like, but I was unfulfilled. I began to question whether services full of people equated to being successful. I asked myself, *Is winning new people to Jesus the goal, or are we just enjoying church for ourselves?* I thought serving God in this particular way at this specific church was supposed to be my destiny, but why did I feel discontent in my heart? What was this gnawing in the pit of my stomach that was making me feel unsettled and unsatisfied?

There was no issue with the church that my parents were leading; the issue was within me. The passion that God had put inside me as a child was coasting in the current of my parents' calling, and it was good and comfortable for me until it became uncomfortable. Over the years, I've learned that discomfort usually indicates that a shift is coming.

I thought, *Isn't this what God called us to as a family? We are doing work for Jesus, the church is growing, we bought a new building. Shouldn't I feel more content? After all, we are doing good things, right?*

If I'm honest, I spent many years believing the discontent I felt meant that my parents were doing something wrong with their approach to ministry. The vision God had given my parents was specific to them and they were obedient to that. As I matured, I could see the bigger picture and appreciate our differences and the beauty they created operating together. I remember many conversations where my immaturity and my discontented heart judged the church my parents were leading.

Although I wish I could hit the rewind button and undo the hurtful words I said to my parents and others in that season, and the know-it-all mindset that I had, I can't. Our differences were obvious, but we are family. I have repented to God, made amends with my parents, and apologized to as many people as possible to acknowledge my errors and immaturity.

As I look back with hindsight bias, I realize the discontent I felt at the time meant that God was calling me to something different. He wasn't calling me to something better; He was setting me apart for something that simply hadn't been done before in our church.

DRAWING LINES

Looking back, I can see how everything that God allowed me to experience throughout my youth was setting me apart for a particular service in a specific space. Even as a child I would notice things that other people didn't. I would ask, "Why is that guy living on the street and it seems like nobody cares?" I would ask my dad to pick up different kids on my sports team who didn't have dads because I wanted them to experience what I had with him for themselves. My heart would break for things that I thought other people didn't seem to care about or acknowledge.

Even though we were following Jesus, it felt like we were drawing lines that Jesus never drew, and that didn't make sense to me.

Instead of drawing lines, I was being drawn to people who didn't look, think, or act like me. I was the one who stood up for the kids who were getting bullied. I would put myself in harm's way for any type of injustice. Intervening on behalf of the weak and marginalized was as natural for me at nine years old as it is for me today. It was always difficult for me to grasp the idea that only certain people were invited to the party of popular people while those who were on the outside were excluded.

Status quo, cultural norms, and what people had decided was acceptable or not acceptable created limitations for certain groups of people, and that never sat right with me. Where other people felt comfortable with everyone being the same, I felt concerned by the uniformity. While a lack of diversity was normal and familiar to those around me, it felt abnormal and uncomfortable to me.

People around me seemed to be content to stay inside the lines, but I wasn't content there. I couldn't be. I felt like my job was to love outside the lines.

A VISION IN THE VALLEY

Being stopped in the Great Rift Valley created space for me to consider what God was up to at home. As I sat in the broken-down van, I felt this rift building in my own soul. I was once again in the back seat of a vehicle, just like I had been on those rides to church with my parents, listening to them share about the vision God had given them for their ministry. But this time, instead of drawing against the grain of the blue velvet seats in my dad's Ford LTD, I was typing on a computer the calling God was giving me for my life and ministry.

God was giving me a vision in the valley.

And I sensed it was to be a calling that would go against the grain of the church culture I was used to. I was in the middle of nowhere, but I felt I was right where I was supposed to be.

It's crazy how God brought me all the way to the Great Rift Valley to show me a real-life illustration of the rift I had in my life at the time. I was in a foreign place, having left the comforts of my home country, unfamiliar with where I was but certain of where I was headed, even if I had not seen it before. This was different from any circumstance I had ever been in, but for some reason different felt right. Being in the middle of nowhere was right where God wanted me to be, and I was willing to embrace the discomfort of being disoriented.

In the middle of the Great Rift Valley in Kenya, I was suddenly keenly aware of a second rift in my life: the way I'd expressed my convictions about ministry had caused a rift in my family back home. God was speaking to me about a ministry of reconciliation that I had to first live out in my own family before I could live it out in a greater purpose in the future. I had been the greatest contributor to the rift in my family because I'd misunderstood my call. I was being tested in what it looked like to reconcile differences and failing at it. I had caused a rift in my family, yet God was calling me to be a bridge builder in the family of God. I was called to bring people together, yet I was the one who had brought division.

You see, a rift is "a difference in opinion, belief, or interest that causes such a break" in relationship.[1] And that was exactly what I was creating—a break. I felt my ideas were better and my way was the right and ideal way. God broke me down in the middle of nowhere to get my attention and deal with my heart, which desperately needed a shift in perspective.

My journey to discovering and walking in my God-given purpose would require me to first learn from and navigate my own personal pain. It's in moments like these when our mistakes can be loud and send shaming messages of failure; however, I thank God for His grace and mercy!

I began to see my own biases as I took an honest evaluation of my heart and motivations. This was an opportunity for growth. My prayers went from, "God, change them" to "God, change me!" This was the beginning of God breaking my heart for something that breaks His heart greatly—division and discord. This divine interruption was the breakdown my heart needed to shift direction, recalculate the way ahead, and approach what I felt God's call was from a different perspective.

FATHER ABRAHAM

Growing up I was easily distracted. I had severe ADHD, so every little thing would steal my attention, which made learning really challenging. I realized early on that one of the best ways for me to learn was through music and nursery rhymes. Something would be difficult for me to understand, but if it had a melody, I could sing the tune over and over again until the words became a part of my heart.

One of the songs I remember resonating with me from a young age was "Father Abraham":

> *Father Abraham had many sons*
> *Many sons had Father Abraham*
> *I am one of them and so are you*
> *So let's just praise the Lord*[2]

Abraham is one of the heroes of the faith. We call him Father Abraham in the song because this movement that now spans across so many different tribes, tongues, and nations started with him. It started with Abraham saying yes to leaving his comfort zone and going into an unknown place. That song resonated with me because it's about the crazy steps of faith Abraham took to move outside the lines previous generations had drawn.

The story begins in Genesis 12:1–3:

> The LORD had said to Abram, "Leave your native country, your relatives, and your father's family, and go to the land

that I will show you. I will make you into a great nation. I will bless you and make you famous, and you will be a blessing to others. I will bless those who bless you and curse those who treat you with contempt. All the families on earth will be blessed through you." (NLT)

I can only imagine how Abraham felt when God asked him to do what may have seemed unreasonable at the time. Abraham was comfortable where he was, but God had a bigger agenda than just blessing Abraham's house, his family, or even the geographic location where Abraham's family lived. This was not about what God wanted to do *for* Abraham but rather what He wanted to do *through* Abraham. Can you imagine that conversation between God and Abraham?

In my mind's eye the conversation goes something like this: The phone rings. "Hey, Abe! It's Me, God!"

"Oh, hey, God," Abraham responds.

"Listen, I have something that I want to do in the earth, and I was thinking, who could I send to handle such a monumental task and carry out My plan?" (I can picture Abraham's anxiety rising in real time every time I read this passage.)

"So here's the deal," God continues. "I made this huge promise when I created mankind. I promised My power, provision, and protection. Well, it was actually more of a covenant."

If I had been in Abraham's shoes, I probably would have been thinking, *What does this have to do with me?*

God begins to explain how He spoke Adam and Eve into existence and gave them authority over the animals. "They were completely in charge of everything. I gave them all of this because of My great love for them. They were living their best lives!"

"Um, God, what does this have to do with me?"

"Well, Abe, to make a long story short, I told them that everything in this garden was at their disposal except for one particular tree. I told them that they would surely die if they ate from that tree, but the temptation was great, and they ended up eating the fruit anyway. It was at that moment that I had to cut them off, but they had no idea that their disobedience would affect generations to come. When Adam sinned, sin entered the world. Adam's sin brought death, so death spread to everyone, for everyone sinned. But because of My great love for mankind, I cannot allow the curse of sin to be a death sentence from generation to generation. Abe, you still there?"

"Yes, God, I'm still here."

"I want you to help Me fix this. I love man too much to let this go on for too long. I want you to help Me restore My relationship with My people. I will make you a great nation. I will bless you and I will make your name great. I will even bless those who bless you along the journey and curse those who do anything to stop you from carrying out My love mission to restore our relationship. I want you to know, Abraham, that through you all the families of the earth will be blessed. And guess what, Abraham—I'm going to equip you with everything you will need along the way."

I can imagine Abraham's excitement, hearing how the God of heaven and earth wants to use him. Abraham replies, "God, this is absolutely amazing that You want to use me to carry out such a holy assignment to restore Your relationship with Your people. I'm all in! When do I start?"

In that moment I'm sure Abraham began to realize what was required of him personally in order for him to fulfill God's call publicly. This great call from God did not come without a great cost. This new destination Abraham was about to set out for required sacrifice. God said, "Leave your native country, your relatives, and your father's family" (Genesis 12:1 NLT). In other words, it's time to move past all the boundaries and borders you grew up in—it's time to move outside the lines.

Abraham had to be willing to let go of what was in order to explore the possibilities of what could be. He had to be willing to change his present location so that God could change future generations.

I'm sure the conversation with Abraham's family and his countrymen felt uncomfortable. However, being uncomfortable with his family was exactly what God needed to set a new coordinate for their future. A new breakthrough required testing old boundaries. You see, Abraham's father and grandfather were known for worshiping idols. An idol is anything we decide to put in God's place. It's anything we want to hold on to that God wants us to let go of. We can make an idol out of the places where we're living, the careers we're pursuing, or the ideologies we're holding. Whenever we worship an idol, we are settling for less than God's best. That's what Abraham was up against. The two generations before him had decided to settle short of what God had for them. But God was raising up Abraham as a pioneer to push past the boundaries of generational expectations and step out as a benchmark of faith for a new future.

God told Abraham it was time to do something new. He was going to make Abraham and his descendants into a great nation that would bless all the people on the earth (Genesis 12:2–3). God was calling Abraham to bless everyone, not just the people who looked like him or thought like him. But in order to get there, Abraham first had to leave the lines he was comfortable with. He had to be willing to step outside the boundaries his family had created.

Abraham answered this call with faith, confidence, and a deep conviction that honoring the call on his life might mean leaving his family. But leaving his family was not dishonoring his family. Rather it was building upon the legacy of what had gone before him.

I now understand that the call to bring a divided man back into relationship with God sometimes requires separation from those we love. Abraham had to step away from the place and the people he grew up with. But his obedience put the whole story of the Bible—the story of God restoring and redeeming relationships—into motion.

Abraham crossed over the lines that the generations before him had drawn. He crossed over the boundaries and loved outside the lines. He set the standard for what it looks like to go to people and places that are outside our comfort zones. And today kids from all walks of life are still singing about how we are all his sons and daughters.

This call to love outside the lines is a call to all of us as God's children. I believe that God is asking every last one of His children to answer His call as Abraham did. For years I heard many preachers shout from the stage, "We are the seed of Abraham! What God promised Abraham, He also promised us." But we can't just take in Abraham's promise; we have to walk out Abraham's purpose. We have to put our mission where our mouths have been.

The apostle Paul is a great example of someone who erased lines. He was constantly fighting to take the church to more and more people groups around the world, always fighting to expand and bring everyone into the family. He said it this way: "For you are all children of God through faith in Christ Jesus. And all who have been united with Christ in baptism have put on Christ, like putting on new clothes. There is no longer Jew or Gentile, slave or free, male and female. For you are all one in Christ Jesus. And now that you belong to Christ, you are the true children of Abraham. You are his heirs, and God's promise to Abraham belongs to you" (Galatians 3:26-29 NLT).

We are Abraham's descendants, and it's our job to join in the same chorus Abraham sang. A chorus of unity. A chorus of diversity. We must have hearts that are big enough to love people from many nations. Many colors. Many creeds.

Through Abraham, God shows us that we are all a part of one family. Father Abraham had many sons, and we are called to fight for unity with every one of them.

As sons and daughters, it's our job to follow in Abraham's footsteps. We need to step over the boundaries and borders we are comfortable with and begin to build relationships with people who don't look the same as us.

We need to love outside the lines.

WE ARE FAMILY

Growing up, it was a tradition that our entire extended family would get together during the summer for a family reunion. Everybody would fix their best side dish, bring it all together, and fellowship over a bountiful buffet.

The side dishes were amazing, but they were nothing like the main course. The main course was always a table covered with the freshest Maryland blue crab you have ever seen. Everybody would come, not only to see old and new faces but to take part in the endless all-you-can-eat crab, beef, and ribs.

At these reunions I remember being introduced to cousins and aunts I had never seen before. The only reason I knew they were family was because everyone had on a purple T-shirt that said: "We are family!"

The purple shirts unified our diverse faces from diverse places with diverse backgrounds and various skin tones. I never knew I had so much family. And when someone showed up without the T-shirt, my auntie always had extras in the trunk of her car, ready to quickly make outsiders feel like insiders and a part of the family.

That's a great picture of what God calls us to do. Because we live in a fallen world, we let skin color, language, and even personal preferences divide us. We let our differences keep us from coming together and realizing we are a part of the same family. The Bible says that God "has clothed me with the garments of salvation; he has covered me with the robe of righteousness" (Isaiah 61:10 ESV). Just like our family passed around those purple T-shirts to acknowledge that we were family, we get to pass down the garments of salvation from generation to generation to remember that we are part of a much bigger family.

When I read the begats in the book of Matthew, I realize that without Abraham's sacrifice there could be no Jesus sacrifice. Abraham is the father of the faith and Jesus is the Son of salvation. Abraham's assignment was to reunite man with God's covenant. I believe we are in the era of Abraham, and it is also our purpose to continually bring a man separated from God back to oneness with God.

Abraham's call from God happened a long time ago, but I believe that God hit the redial button thousands of years later for us to continue to live out that call through our lives in Christ Jesus. Abraham was told that all the people of the world would be blessed through him. Think about that for a second. The world is a diverse place. So in order for Abraham to embrace his assignment of unity, he had to embrace different faces and cultures. God took him out of his comfort zone and brought him to lands he had never been to and people he had never met.

My family may be big, but Abraham's is bigger. My family may be diverse, but his is as diverse as they come. God's family is from all different nations, and it's our job to reach outside the lines we've created and love them.

Why?

Because Abraham didn't stay within the lines—he made a departure. He left his father's house and his country to extend his family beyond what they had settled for.

ANSWER THE CALL

Have you ever felt the urgency to get a message to a friend or family member? A message so critical that you would not stop until it was received? That's the urgency we see in Scripture when God called individuals to do the work He had for them. The call was a specific message from God for a specific assignment for God.

Throughout Scripture, when God had a specific task or an assignment, He spoke to people, He called people. He put the burden for a specific situation into a specific person's soul. The call was God's invitation to a particular person to join Him on His mission.

The call of God is an assignment. It's something God wants His people to do or the earth to experience. Examples of these calls are found all throughout Scripture with all the great biblical heroes.

Moses was an outcast raised by an adoptive family and was an unlikely candidate to be God's mouthpiece and go before Pharaoh to demand he let God's people go. Moses had the ringer on as God unveiled Himself through a burning bush and recruited him in the mission to end over four hundred years of slavery and oppression of God's people.

David was not known to be in the public eye, as he spent countless days in the wilderness tending sheep and fighting off predators. But one day he was taking grilled cheese sandwiches to his brothers, who were fighting a battle, and he overheard trash talk coming from a giant named Goliath. David's phone was ringing; God was calling, and he answered.

Then there was an unlikely, unknown biblical character named Jael. God called her to preserve the lineage of Jesus hundreds of years before the reality of Jesus. The commander of the Canaanite army was a man named Sisera, who had terrorized God's people for over twenty years. When the Hebrew commander, Barak, hesitated to take God's call, God called a woman who was a tent dweller to use what she had at her disposal to take out Sisera. The call was subtle, but her answer was blaring.

And when God called Abraham out from his family, his country, and his father's house, he went. He heard the call, picked up the phone, and immediately left everything to pursue God's purpose of bringing unity back to God's people.

Years ago, as I sat in the van in the middle of the Great Rift Valley, I realized God was suddenly calling me once again just as He had when I was a child. He was saying, *Jimmy, answer the phone. I have a need in the earth that I want you to help Me with.* I could no longer ignore the redial of redirection. My resounding yes was followed by my commitment to spend the rest of my life doing everything I can to bridge the rift in my biological family and the rifts all over the world in my spiritual family.

God wasn't looking for my opinion; He was looking for my obedience.

Our world is divided, but God is looking for men and women who are ready to step over those divisions and bring unity. It's time to answer the phone. Whether you've ignored the subtle vibration of God gently calling you or the loud ringing caused by watching heartbreaking events continue to cause rifts in our country and our world, it's time. God is calling you to be someone who steps over boundaries and borders and loves outside the lines.

This book is going to equip you to do that, but first you must be willing to say yes. Are you ready to answer the call?

A NEW VISION

The ache of the rift was getting stronger and stronger, and I was typing faster and faster. The moment became divine. God was stepping into my rift and speaking to it.

I started to type up a vision of a new way of doing church: instead of being a church that does outreach, let's be an outreach powered by a church. A place where White, Black, Latino, Native American, Asian, and all people came together to worship God and serve the city. A place where Christianity was not defined by going to a service but by being a service. A place where we were less concerned with what someone wore on their bodies and more passionate about what was carried in their hearts. A place where we valued diversity and were willing to sacrifice our preferences to reach anybody and everybody.

And most importantly, a place where we knew that the vision

was about something far bigger than a church building. Church doesn't start when the service begins; it starts when the service ends. Because this message is not just for those within the four walls of the church; it's for the four corners of the earth.

Sitting in the back of a van in the Great Rift Valley, God gave me a divine download, a vision that spoke to the rift in my soul.

God still wanted me to build the church, but to go in a different direction. He was using this rift in my soul to call me to a detour. At that moment, I began to realize that God was present not only there in the Rift Valley but also in the rift I felt back home. He was calling me to be a bridge builder. He was recalculating my direction from my comfort, from church tradition, and from the cultural norm.

Just as with Abraham taking new territory, I had to be willing to sacrifice a few sacred cows along the way and push over a few pink elephants (the obvious things that needed to change) on a journey to a greater future. He was calling me to follow Him on a path into the unknown of a divine destination. Once again, through all of this, God did not want my opinion; He wanted my obedience.

Rifts and struggles are natural parts of life, and many times they are born out of growth. In the face of this rift—the struggle, crack, or break in the shalom, or peace, God intends for the world He loves—Jesus invites His disciples to repair the breach. The question we'll be asking on this journey is not, What is happening to us? but, What does God intend to do through us?

Lines are unnecessary boundaries we draw between one another based on race, difference, or preference. We all draw lines. But God is calling you and me to build His kingdom by loving outside the lines. It is a call to lead in love, to have hard conversations, to forgive and educate, and to learn from Jesus how to live beyond ourselves, love beyond our preferences, and laugh beyond our struggles.

Can you hear the call?

Are you ready to carry love across boundaries? Are you ready to own your role as a bridge builder? Carrying our love outside the lines means we can't let the voices of division cause us to drift to one side or the other. We must stay attuned to the voice in the valley. The voice that calls us to be open to God transforming our lives so that we can carry love outside the lines. So that we can make disciples of those who bring division. To make followers of Jesus those who have been led by feelings of hate or injustice. To allow the call of God to overtake the noise of contentiousness and fear.

My prayer as you read the words on these pages is that you will hear God's voice in our world's Rift Valley and join me to discover God's destiny as we learn to love outside the lines.

Let's journey together!

—————————— HEART CHECK ——————————

- As you read this chapter, what did God reveal to you about your own heart?
- Do you notice any rifts in your own family or church community? What is one thing you can do today to bring some healing to that divide?

23

- God called Abraham to step outside his usual boundaries. What are some lines God may be calling you to step over, and who are some people God may be calling you to?

God, You called Abraham to step across the lines and move outside his comfort zone, and now, I pray that You would call me to do the same thing. Lord, I pray that You would help me acknowledge the internal rifts in my own heart and the external rifts all around me that break Your heart. Help me see where I am causing division in my own home or in my community of friends, and give me the strength to carry Your love into those places.

---------------------- TWO ----------------------

FAMILY DISCUSSIONS

*When we confess our history, it gives us
the ability to profess a new hope.*

**When I was growing up, the dining room in our home was
off-limits.** The room was situated between the kitchen and the
living room and had this giant, beautiful wooden table in the
center. But there were only two occasions when we were allowed
to sit at that table.

The first was when all our family was in town for a
Thanksgiving or Christmas meal. When the whole family was
together, the table that typically sat empty would be packed full
of food, and we would laugh, celebrate, and eat way too much.

The only other occasion when we were allowed to sit at the
dining room table was whenever two of us got into a fight. When

my sister and I started arguing, or my cousins and I got in a heated debate, my mom would call us into the dining room and make us sit down at that wooden table for what she would call a "family discussion."

I'll never forget those conversations. When Mom called for a family discussion, it wasn't optional. We weren't allowed to consider whether we wanted to sit down and talk, and we weren't leaving the table until we all worked it out.

"We are going to sit at this table until we start acting like family," she would say. "I don't care who's right or who's wrong; we are not leaving this table until this is resolved. We are family. Now tell me what happened."

Sometimes I wasn't even the one involved in the division. My sister and one of our cousins would get into an argument, but since I was family, I'd still have to sit at that wooden dining room table and listen as they worked it out.

Family discussions were uncomfortable.

At first everyone would bring anger, fear, and resentment to the table. One of us would be upset about something another said or did, and in our anger, we'd want to draw a line and exclude that person from our life. But my mom refused to let us draw lines between family. Instead she made us sit with one another and talk it out until the resentment slowly turned into understanding. Eventually we'd go from being frustrated with each other to realizing that we are family, and although families fight sometimes, they eventually work it out and stick together.

And so the dining room table was forbidden, except for when family was together to celebrate or was divided by a fight. My mom understood that something amazing happens when you sit down and listen to each other. When you take the time to hear someone else's perspective, it allows you to empathize with their emotions.

Those family discussions are what this chapter is all about.

In chapter 1 we established that we are family. When you put on that garment of salvation, it means you are a part of a giant and diverse family. And that means we come to the table together to celebrate. But it also means that when there is division, we sit down and talk about it. Because we are family, and we don't have another option. When you are family, you talk things out. You don't let pain, anger, or bitterness create division. You don't let hate divide. And wherever lines have been drawn, you sit down and try to hear both perspectives until the lines disappear.

There is division in our world. Lines have been drawn. And as the family of God, it's our job to sit at the table and have a family discussion about them. Whether you feel like you are a part of that pain or not, we are family, which means we all have the responsibility to at least show up and listen.

FAMILY HISTORY

I've had a lot of surgeries in my life. One was for my knee, another for my gallbladder, but most of them have been for my back. My back has had a lot of problems and a lot of pain throughout the years, so I've spent a lot of time in doctors' offices.

My least favorite part about going to the doctor is filling out that giant form before going in. Every time I sit down to answer the questions, I look around at everyone else scribbling away, and I wonder when doctors' offices are going to catch up with the times and go digital.

What's even more frustrating is that the questions on the form never seem to have anything to do with why I am there. They are all about my history, the different surgeries I've had on different body parts, or the different medications I take. Part of me just wants to write: *What does any of this have to do with my back?*

But then it gets worse. The farther down the giant form I go, the questions stop being about me and instead become about my family.

My family? What does my family have to do with my back pain?

Maybe it was the pain in my back talking, but one day I got fed up, stopped filling out the form, and asked the doctor what any of this had to do with my pain. My doctor told me something really interesting. The doctor told me they could learn a lot about my problem and what I'm dealing with by looking at my family lineage.

The same thing is true in this conversation we're having about learning to love outside the lines. This book is about learning to understand people who don't share our ideologies, who haven't experienced our generational norms, and who erect boundaries that block us from certain groups of people. But if we want to move past these walls that are keeping us divided, we first must understand where they came from.

The first thing we usually realized in all of our family discussions is that the incident that caused the pain didn't happen in a vacuum. There was always a backstory to the behavior, a history of events that led up to the fight between me and my sister or cousin. The first step in having a successful family discussion was always being willing to notice all the pain from the past that was leading up to the present pain.

Because the thing about these lines is most of us didn't invent them—we inherited them. Our lines come from our lineage. No one is born believing ugly stereotypes about others. No one is born racist. No one is born a rioting hater—it's a learned behavior. And unfortunately, we've been passing on these learned behaviors for thousands of years. Line drawing is in our lineage, and everyone picks up some form of it along the way.

We must be willing to look back on our history and be honest about where the division came from. Our family lines drew lines, and it's caused a lot of pain for a lot of people. As we realize our past and put in the work to listen to stories of the division, we'll realize our line and our family caused us to both knowingly and unknowingly draw lines in our present. History is not meant to hurt us and take us back; it's meant to heal us and move us forward. But in order to accept a new destiny, we must acknowledge an old history.

You are reading this book because you are acknowledging that we are in pain. But fixing this pain starts the same way every doctor visit starts. We have to be willing to fill out that giant form that talks about our family history.

LINES IN OUR LINEAGE

I grew up in a suburban, middle-class neighborhood. Although my family may not have had what a lot of our neighbors had, I didn't grow up feeling a strong racial divide.

All my friends were White, but I never thought about that. And we never talked about it. As I think back on it, I remember noticing that our parents didn't hang out together or sit with one another in the football stands, but we never thought about how I was Black and they were White. As kids we didn't draw lines. We weren't divided. We all just got along.

But all of that changed for me one day in my sixth-grade history class.

We opened up our history books, and there was a picture of a slave with a noose around his neck. The history book we were using had the N-word in it, in more than one place. At the time I was one of two Black kids in my class. I was so uncomfortable because there were kids giggling at the picture. That was the moment the plates began to shift under the surface in my mind, and I realized the rift: we may have lived on the same earth and attended the same schools, but my White classmates and I lived in completely different worlds. In my world the picture signaled a horror; in another person's world, it was a joke.

I was paralyzed by that picture. It harmed my friendships with my White friends. Their laughter was more the result of ignorance than evil intent, but they were still laughing. And it made me feel like I was less than them.

As I stared at that picture, everything started to change. I became aware of the division. I began to see the pain that has divided our country from the beginning. Suddenly the lines in our lineage became painfully evident.

CHECK IN

That picture still haunts me. All these years later I still think about that moment. And before we race off to the next chapter, would you just sit with that story for a second? That was my experience.

Now here's the question: What happened in your heart as you read that story?

Was your first thought about those children who laughed? *Well, I didn't do that. That wasn't me.*

Did you want to distinguish yourself as being different from those who were racially insensitive? Because the first key to having a successful family discussion is getting to the point where we can listen to someone else's perspective and pain without getting defensive. The first step is to be able to listen without judging or justifying.

What is your response to seeing another suffering injustice? Each of us has a choice in how we respond when we witness something we know is not right. Our feelings are shaped by our perceptions and what we think about what we see.

My daughter and I can sit and watch the same dramatic movie. If it gets too quiet, and I look at her and she is crying over the movie, I will say, "Are you serious? It's not real!" Same movie, two different feelings. In her mind she has either become one of the characters or it has connected to an experience that she has had in real life. Either way, in her thoughts, what has played out to her has become real, and she feels sad.

Across the same couch, I'm there because I wanted to spend time with my girl. I have no investment in the characters, and the plot means nothing to me. In my mind none of this is real, and I feel nothing. Actually I do feel. I feel confused as to why I let her choose the movie in the first place and would like nothing more than for it to be over so I can get my remote back.

This is simple and pretty normal father and daughter behavior, right? But what is your response when you read that story about me in sixth-grade history class? Does it move you? Are you like my daughter, who places herself in the situation and sees it from the character's point of view? Or are you like me, telling yourself this isn't real and finding yourself confused by those who are making you see this?

What are you thinking when you are watching? What are those thoughts based on? Are they based on what you were taught growing up? Something else you saw on TV? Do you try to understand it based on your experience or opinions, or do you seek to understand more? Are you trying to process someone else's experience based on your own, or do you try to look at something beyond yourself?

When you watch the news and hear about all the division in our country and in our world, what are your thoughts? Do you see those issues as problems that those people over there need to fig- ure out? When you hear judicial verdicts on the news, especially ones that are racially charged, do you allow them to impact you personally, or do you hold them at arm's length? When you hear about divisions, do you see them as other people's problems, or do you see family problems?

Is your first thought, *They should probably have a discussion about that*?

Or is it, *We need to have a family discussion about this*?

When it comes to our lineage of drawing lines, we cannot change the channel, hit Pause, or turn off the TV. And our attempts to do so have made us more divided than unified.

We need to be willing to stay present in this family conversation, because a lot of this stuff we are dealing with is family lineage. Are you aware of the racism that exists in your family lineage? We need to stop ignoring it and let history be a part of our healing.

Our nation has experienced centuries of division, and these lines go all the way back to the beginning. If we really want to heal, the doctor is going to need all our family history, so let's go all the way back to the beginning—to the first two humans to ever live.

BOUNDARIES FROM THE BEGINNING

Adam and Eve were the first in a long line of division.

In the previous chapter we talked about how they were naked and unashamed in the garden with only one rule: to stay away from the forbidden fruit. But they couldn't do it. Once they ate the fruit, things fell apart.

After that the story tells us about the consequences of their actions. God went straight to Adam and asked, "Who told you that you were naked? Have you eaten from the tree that I commanded you not to eat from?" (Genesis 3:11 WEB).

In that moment Adam had an opportunity to come clean. He could have just confessed and told God what they had done, but instead, he chose division and said, "The woman you put here with me. . . . She gave me some of the fruit, and I ate it" (Genesis 3:12 CEV).

And so the blame game began. When God asked Eve the same question, she said, "The serpent deceived me, and I ate" (Genesis 3:13 ESV).

Adam blamed Eve. Eve blamed the Serpent. And blame always leads us to set up borders and boundaries. It turned the unity that Adam and Eve were meant to experience into division. These boundaries have been up from the very beginning. The lines are in our lineage, and they have been passed down to every generation.

I have seen so many commercials with advertisements trying to get people to buy DNA tests to see where they come from and to research their family trees. And if I'm honest that sort of thing has never really mattered to me because I always think, *What does that change?*

But knowing our history can change our authority. Knowing our lineage speaks to a much greater legacy. In order to redeem what happened to Adam and Eve in Eden when they ate from the forbidden tree, we are going to have to embrace our spiritual family trees. Because Adam and Eve weren't the only ones who suffered from this division—so has every generation that has followed.

DESTINED FOR DIVISION

Genesis 3 describes a division between Adam and Eve, and Genesis 4 unpacks how that division was passed down to the next generation.

Cain and Abel were two brothers who lived for God but had conflict. Cain was a farmer; Abel was a shepherd. Cain was older; Abel was younger. Cain brought an inadequate offering of his crops as a gift to the Lord; Abel brought the best of what he had to the Lord. Abel's gifts were accepted by God; Cain's gifts were not.

God spoke to Cain in the midst of his struggle and offered him an opportunity. God said, "You will be accepted if you do what is right. But if you refuse to do what is right, then watch out! Sin is crouching at the door, eager to control you. But you must subdue it and be its master" (Genesis 4:7 NLT).

Cain had a choice. He wasn't so far from God that he didn't hear Him; Cain just had to commit to do what he was told to do. Unfortunately Cain did not take that route. He killed his brother, the one that he was chosen to be in a family with by God, the one he was called to worship with by order of birthright.

Instead of sitting down at the dining room table for a family discussion, Cain took matters into his own hands.

Instead of reconciliation, Cain chose division.

Adam and Eve passed on a lineage of drawing lines to their

kids. Sin turned God's design into division. Instead of operating as a unified family, Cain drew a line between him and his brother. They remained divided, and eventually it led to murder. And from there things only got worse.

We could spend the rest of this book talking about the divisions throughout the Old Testament. Even King David, the man after God's own heart, had an affair with his friend Uriah's wife, and then instead of confessing and fighting for unity, he had Uriah killed in battle. In the middle of David's darkest moment, he could've fought for unity, but instead he decided to draw a line between him and Uriah. Sin not only separated David from God but it also separated him from Uriah—cover-ups always cause a chasm. We come from a lineage of line drawers. When you read the Old Testament, it doesn't take long to start to wonder if we are all destined for division for all of eternity.

But if we spent all day writing out our family histories of pain and division, we would need a bigger form and would never make it in to see the doctor. The good news is there is a cure for all this pain.

A NEW DESTINY

Here's the most important part of this family discussion. We may have a lineage of line drawers, but that doesn't mean those lines are our destiny. The division that began with a fruit tree was passed down to generation after generation until Jesus stepped in and hung on another tree so that we could go free. Galatians

3:13 says, "But Christ has rescued us from the curse pronounced by the law. When he was hung on the cross, he took upon himself the curse for our wrongdoing. For it is written in the Scriptures, 'Cursed is everyone who is hung on a tree'" (NLT).

Scripture reminds us that although we come from a lineage of line drawers, Jesus stepped in and laid down His life so that we could begin to write a different story. Jesus came to bring a new destiny to division. He came to bring new life to an old lineage. Jesus came to absolve the sins of Adam and Eve.

Fam, now is the moment to gather up at the table, notice and name the lines, and then love beyond them. This new life is possible for you to experience today. The Bible says only two things are required from us to experience it: confession and belief. Romans 10:9 says, "If you declare with your mouth, 'Jesus is Lord,' and believe in your heart that God raised him from the dead, you will be saved."

There is power in confession. Confession is a current profession of a past issue. Confession is what leads us to restoration in Christ. Confession also helps restore our relationships with one another.

Our family discussions would usually end with one of us apologizing. Sometimes it took us a while to get there, but eventually we'd end up bringing the hurtful things we said or did to each other to the light, owning the pain we caused, and saying, "I'm sorry."

That's where the power is. That's where walls start to fall down and the lines that stand between us start to lose their grip. That's why James 5:16 says, "Confess your sins to one another and pray for one another, that you may be healed" (ESV).

Part of the old things being passed away is acknowledging that those old things happened—records matter. If we go back and look at the track record, we can heal from the pain of those old things. We must embrace history because where we are is a result of where we've been.

Our history can motivate us to do better. Our past can inspire us toward a new destiny. But first we must confess our history. When we confess our history, it gives us the ability to profess a new hope.

LEARN TO LISTEN

Filling out those forms for the doctor wasn't fun, but it was really helpful for my provider and beneficial for me. It helped the doctor to understand the pain I was feeling and know the right questions to ask me.

As many forms as I've filled out, I've never once had any doctor try to negotiate away my level of pain. There is something beautiful about that picture. The doctors never said, "Are you sure it really hurts there? Are you sure your pain level is an eight? Isn't it really just a one?"

Good doctors learn how to listen to their patients' pain without judging it. They don't get defensive. My doctors didn't try to convince me that they weren't responsible for causing my back pain. They just listened to what I was experiencing and then prescribed me the right cure for the pain.

I wonder if we are being too quick to try to write prescriptions for people without first being willing to sit and listen to their pain. It's a lot easier to jump to conclusions and throw out quick fixes than it is to sit, listen, and empathize, then work toward a solution together. I don't believe we can really move forward in unity and healing from division unless we are able to listen to people's pain.

When we hear other people's stories, it's not an indictment on us; it's an opportunity for us to step into their history and learn to listen. It's a chance for us to experience their pain and empathize with their pain. In order to love outside the lines, we have to look into the lineage.

Families may have disagreements, but we never settle for disunity.

In this process we are going to have grace for one another, and we are going to remember the same lesson my mom taught me all those years ago: family discussions may be uncomfortable, but we are in this together. We are family, and ultimately family discussions are about restoring unity.

So let's keep going, and let's lean in and get ready for the rest of this book. This call to love outside the lines is going to cost us something, but I know you are up for the challenge.

HEART CHECK

- What emotions were you feeling during the family discussion in this chapter?
- What lines do you have in your lineage? Who are people that your family, through the generations, has considered to be "other"?

- Who is one person that is outside the artificial lines your culture has drawn that you could learn to listen to this week? What would it look like to call them, ask them about their experience, and then just take time to listen instead of responding?

Father, thank You that we are all a part of one family—Your family. Family discussions are not always easy, but they are so important, so give me the love, grace, and courage I need to have them today. Help me to see the people in my life that I have hurt or misunderstood, and give me the boldness I need to erase the lines I have formed. Line drawing may be in my past, but I pray it would not be in my future.

THREE

SELLOUT OR SOLD OUT?

*Your ethnic culture is now a subculture
to the kingdom culture.*

A few years ago our neighbors installed an invisible fence for their dog. The dog wasn't big or dangerous, but he was full of energy and would often take off at a sprint down the street. We watched as the natural exploratory impulse of this new family member was controlled and limited by what he could not see.

This invisible fence was simply an unseen boundary buried underground along the property line. This boundary would send a shock to the dog's collar whenever the dog would get too close to the property line. Although the boundaries were unseen, they were most definitely felt by every jarring shock of his electric collar each time the wonder of newness and the temptation of curiosity got the best of him.

Its purpose was to train this new family member to not stray too far from the family's home. It was to keep him only within the designated territory and the confines of what was safe for those within the unseen perimeter and those on the other side of the unseen fence. From the outside looking in, I could see how this was an effective method of training their new puppy. I could also see the pain the dog experienced when going beyond what others had decided was safe.

Life is full of boundaries—some seen, some unseen. Some spoken, some unspoken. Boundaries are essential when they are used to protect us; however, they can also hurt us. Boundaries harm us when they are used to keep us divided from one another and not unified, especially when it is an unspoken or unseen boundary. When its purpose is to keep us apart, it is then no longer just a boundary. It has become a stronghold that keeps us from experiencing the blessings of relationship that God has purposed for us.

Let's talk about strongholds for a moment. If you've spent much time at church, you've probably heard that word used, but it's rarely defined. The definition of a stronghold is "a place that has been secured tightly in case of attack," or "a place where a particular belief or ideology is firmly believed and staunchly defended."[1]

But the spiritual definition is even more important. A stronghold is a lie, an accusation the Enemy plants in the minds of believers that is contrary to the Word of God.

It's okay to have strong beliefs and opinions, but we must constantly ask the question, Is this rooted in God's Word? Are our opinions, our ideologies, and our stereotypical cultural norms based on Scripture? If the answer is no, those strong opinions can easily become strongholds. Throughout the course of this book, we are going to talk about breaking these strongholds, but first we must identify them, because you can't break what you can't see.

Do you have any invisible fences in your life? Any strongholds that keep you away from other ethnic groups? Take a moment to really think about it.

Maybe you have gone out to lunch with a coworker of a different ethnic background, and you got a funny look from the people who look like you when you got back to work. Words were not said, but it was inferred: *Why were you hanging out with that person? How come you didn't go to lunch with us?* You unknowingly just stepped outside of the invisible fence.

Or perhaps you invite your child's friends of another race to your house for a birthday party and some of your family members are acting a little off because of it. No one comes out and actually says anything, but the guests you welcomed feel less than welcomed by those inside the fence. You just stepped outside the underground boundaries.

Maybe your gym playlist is outside the boundaries of what your friends listen to. Or maybe the sport you play has you in close proximity to people you are not "supposed" to fit with.

I experienced some of these invisible fences in high school, when belonging and acceptance seem to matter most. At that time the expectation of my group of friends was that we had to listen to hip-hop, wear parachute pants like MC Hammer and a Starter jacket (this was the early '90s), and we could only be friends with people who looked like us and did what we did. It was these unspoken expectations, these underlying boundaries that were never verbalized, that bothered me deeply. Hobbies like skateboarding and sports like lacrosse or even baseball—considered by some in my community to be what "they" do—were out of the question. Engaging in these activities came with not only a cost but also a label: *sellout!*

This was the name that was given to those who stepped outside the boundaries or ventured past the limitations of cultural norms. To be a sellout meant that you forgot your roots, your familiarity, your yard, and exchanged it for someone else's. It was understood that if you "leave the yard"—if you leave the safety of the group or hang with "those people"—you were either a traitor or a fake.

In his book *The Third Option*, Miles McPherson puts language to this idea of "selling out." He talks about our natural tendency to form in-groups and out-groups, which creates an us-versus-them mentality.

My group had a culture to which everyone was expected to ascribe. But when someone stopped thinking that way, they were viewed as a sellout who had gone over to the other side.

This works both ways. We had White people in our in-group in high school who were labeled sellouts by other White people because they liked the same things my friends and I liked. They weren't supposed to like hip-hop, their jeans were supposed to be skinnier, and they were supposed to surf after school instead of hanging out with us. When they migrated to join our in-group, they were labeled sellouts by their previous in-group.

As I have journeyed through my life, I have seen people from all walks of life live with invisible fences. The color of our skin is the easy one. But we also let our differences and our preferences create fences. For example, I don't understand people who like their steak well-done. It doesn't make any sense to me; I prefer mine medium-rare. Which isn't that big of a deal, but if I'm not careful, I can let something as inconsequential as steak put an invisible fence between me and others.

Although these fences are often unseen, the effects are glaring. An unwillingness to test the confines of generational boundaries is stifling our country and limiting the call to be one nation under God. These invisible fences are slowly lulling us to sleep and robbing the potential of what life could be if we came together.

Underground boundaries and invisible cultural fences start out subtle but have shocking effects of division and stereotypical thinking that only widen the gap of disunity.

Oftentimes boundaries exist to keep us safe, and some are necessary. But I have come to the realization that a lot of underlying boundaries are not the kind of boundaries created for safety or protection; they are generational strongholds created out of fear and past pain that keep us bound. Who said that you can't be deeply knit to your own family and also call someone on the other side of the fence family? Who said that embracing others means we must let go of us? Does loving them mean that

I'm a sellout to us? Does hanging out or going out to lunch with those people mean that I'm abandoning "our people"? I think the answer is a resounding no!

The very idea of these underlying boundaries was always offensive to me and still is today. What we do, who we love, what music we like or don't like doesn't have to define who we are. And it certainly doesn't have to separate us from others. I think it is time to dig up the fences that separate us and begin constructing bridges that bring us together.

SELLOUT?

Now that I'm older I realize that the safety in familiarity many of us felt as teens or in our younger years is not necessarily safe.

We may stay together but we are still marginalized. And with each public, nationally televised injustice, it feels like the gap gets wider and wider as our world gets smaller and smaller. I have decided that I will not accept these invisible boundaries! And anytime I see someone who is paralyzed by the comfort that comes from staying in their own yard, I plan to continue to offer a little encouragement to move outside their comfort zone and expand their lines. Even in my determination I realize that I still get tested. Each comment is like a buzz in my ear:

"Why do you have so many White friends?"

"Why are you going to preach at *their* church?"

"Why is your church singing those songs?"

No one is directly calling me a sellout. And that's fair, because the old Jimmy would have knocked them out if they said that to my face. But thank God I've come a long way since then. I'm learning to love outside the lines even to people who are still inside the lines. No, the accusations are always more subtle. It's the looks on their faces and their body language letting me know they've got their invisible fences up.

Especially in these times of division in our country, I have been questioned and called a sellout for the relationships I have maintained. I have to work to build bridges in these moments. And the challenge often evokes familiar questions within me.

Do I really have to sacrifice the color of my skin to build a bridge?

Do I have to exchange my cultural history for cultural healing?

Do I have to sacrifice relationships with people outside my race in order to "be down"?

Do I have to give up or trade in my Black card to love people who do not look like me?

Do I have to give up my world to step into someone else's world?

I refuse to reject my identity. God created me to be me! And He created you to be you! He created both of us with the characteristics, uniqueness, idiosyncrasies, and even the family and culture that we have. And when we not only accept but love who we are and how God made us, it can lead to a phenomenal equation—"you" plus "me" equals "we." That's what real unity looks like.

I love you.

I love me.

I love who I am.

I love the way God made me and the culture He placed me in.

But throughout the years, I've also learned to love a variety of people from other cultures. I've broadened my definition of family, and it's caused me to evaluate the expectations we put on cultures. If we keep drawing solid lines in our cultural expectations, we will severely limit cultural expressions.

The apostle Paul maintained the strictest standards of Jewish law, to the point where he called for the death of Christians. After Christ took hold of his life, though, he turned around and began serving those he had previously tried to wipe out. Paul, who was once called Saul, talked about this when he said, "I have become all things to all people so that by all possible means I might save some" (1 Corinthians 9:22).

Paul embraced experiencing life from another person's point of view for the sake of the gospel. Paul wasn't a sellout; he was sold out. He didn't switch from one in-group to another; instead he decided it was time to stop seeing the world as us versus them and started inviting everyone to know Jesus. Our job is to do the same. We need to be sold out to the purposes and causes God has created us for. Sold out to bring His people together. Sold out to expose these underlying boundaries that are really strongholds.

I think sometimes we read the Bible and don't fully absorb the context. Do you realize that Saul lived his life similarly to a leader of a hate group today? He acted on hate in the name of religion; he was a part of a sect that sought out a particular group of people and had them arrested, tortured, and killed. Yet he was radically changed. His whole perspective changed when he met Jesus, and his eyes were opened when a man he was trained to hate, a disciple named Ananias, prayed for him.

Would you call Ananias a sellout? No. Ananias was sold out!

He was sold out to obedience to God and in turn was used to open the eyes of one of the most feared men at the time. Then God delivered that man, Paul, and in turn used him to bridge an even wider gap. Paul became sold out and built churches all over. Paul went from killing to strengthening God's people.

We live by teachings today that have roots in people who were sold out enough to live beyond themselves and serve people outside of their circle. That is the kind of company I want to be in, in the company of those who are sold out.

So how do we do that?

Well, you must understand some things that Ananias and Paul understood in order to break through the strongholds of the past. The first and most important thing they understood was that they were identified by the name of Jesus.

The same is true about us. Today the name of Jesus trumps my last name, my generational lineage, and even my worldly inheritance. I see my ties in the family of God as stronger than the ties of my biological family.

I know that may sound like a big statement, but I mean it. And in order to fully understand why I say that, we have to go back and understand the first thing Jesus said when He began His ministry.

THE KINGDOM OF HEAVEN

Jesus began His ministry with these words: "Repent, for the kingdom of heaven has come near" (Matthew 4:17). Jesus came right out of the gate with an invitation to repent, to turn from previous ways and take a better path. The Greek word for "repent" is *metanoia*, which means "to change your mind."[2] Jesus began His ministry by calling on people to start thinking differently, to turn away from the kingdom of the world and realize that the kingdom of heaven had come near.

The kingdom of the world is divided. As we talked about in chapter 2, it's been that way since Adam and Eve ate from the tree. The world tells us to draw lines, set boundaries, form groups, and stay safe by associating with people who are like us.

But the kingdom of heaven works differently than this world.

In Revelation we get a glimpse into heaven, into the end of the story, and it says, "After this I looked, and there before me was a great multitude that no one could count, from every nation, tribe, people and language, standing before the throne and before the Lamb" (7:9). In the kingdom of heaven, there are no lines drawn between nations, there are no boundaries between tribes, and there are no divisions between languages.

Heaven is a picture of one giant, unified, diverse family!

Jesus was bringing the territory of heaven to the territory of earth to expand His family. But in order to expand the family, we first need to expand our thinking. We need to repent and receive a new and more expansive mindset.

So Jesus began His ministry by inviting us to repent and

change our old (line-drawing) way of thinking to start loving outside the lines. He told us we need a new mindset because the kingdom of heaven is here.

Which means, if you are a follower of Jesus, your ethnic culture is now a subculture to the kingdom culture.

The kingdom of heaven has an agenda, and that agenda is expansion, expectation, and increase. Simply put, God wants us to break down fences that keep people out. He wants us to create a new territory where everyone is a part of the family. That means that your primary agenda is the kingdom agenda—it's to carry God's love over all the lines people draw and invite everyone to know that they are a part of this giant, messy, and diverse family of God.

FOLLOW ME

After Jesus told the world to repent and realize the kingdom of heaven was near, He invited a group of uneducated, ordinary fishermen to join Him on the journey. "Come, follow me," He told them, "and I will send you out to fish for people" (Matthew 4:19).

Think about that for a second. Jesus told them to drop everything they had and the lives they'd been building to follow Him. That's a really big ask. Their nets were the tool they used to make a living, and He invited them to drop them. He told them to put down something that cost them in order to pick up the cause of Christ. Jesus took the disciples on a journey that required them to get outside their comfort zones. They had to decide they wouldn't let the familiarity of what was rob their faith for what could be.

Moving beyond that invisible fence is a radical step, which means it requires radical faith. It can be really uncomfortable, and you don't always know what is going to happen, which means you have to trust and lean on God.

Being sold out requires a trust that is followed up with action and obedience.

You'll discover that necessary mind shifts will only happen when you leave what you are comfortable with. Jesus called His disciples to leave the safety and security of their careers and follow Him.

Trust is the key to obedience.

If we are moving forward without trust, we open the door to fear. We are consumed with thoughts about the worst that could happen. It causes us to run back to the yard, to what is comfortable, because eventually that fear will dictate our actions. When obedience is partnered with trust in God, we are alert in peace, looking for the promises and not for hardship. Trust gives us longevity in obedience and the perspective needed when we cannot see where He is taking us.

What would this look like for you? I suspect that you picked up this book because you are in a place in life where you know there is something more, something better beyond the way you've been living. Maybe you've felt like there is something stopping you but you can't put your finger on what it is. Now you know there is a stronghold you must pass, a boundary to navigate—but how do you do it?

When you listen to Jesus' call and begin to follow Him, you become a new creation. God is giving you a new word for your new jurisdiction, and it is all-inclusive. "If anyone is in Christ, he is a new creation; old things have passed away; behold, all things have become new" (2 Corinthians 5:17 NKJV). All can pass through into this new jurisdiction, this new promise that God has made to us all. All can enjoy a place to live in community with God and all others, not just the ones who look like us. You can have friendships without fear, you can have all people over to your house, you can date outside of your race, you can engage with others and not forget your roots and where you have come from.

Move forward in that knowledge—you are not a sellout; you are sold out for more!

Being sold out is not limited to that initial decision of obedience to step out; being sold out is saying yes to God over and over again. It is a process, a lifelong journey.

Each moment we say yes to God, every time we live beyond ourselves, we are being made. We are being made into something that draws people closer to God and away from the hate and sin that divides us.

For every yes we say to something, we say no to something else. In order to follow, there are things you are going to have to unfollow. The disciples immediately left their nets and boats, but daily they left their egos and their desire for comfort. With each miracle they witnessed they left their worldly logic, and with each person reached they left their preconceived notions about people.

To follow a kingdom agenda and be the type of person who

builds bridges between people, you are going to have to unfollow the world's agenda. To usher in a generation of unity, you are going to have to unfollow a generation of disunity.

Jesus taught this when He was preaching to the masses one day and His immediate family came looking for Him, wanting to talk to Him. He responded, "Here are my mother and my brothers. For whoever does the will of my Father in heaven is my brother and sister and mother" (Matthew 12:49–50). The cost requires you to leave the agenda of the generations before you to follow the agenda of Jesus.

This may require you to speak up at the table when everyone is telling racially or culturally insensitive jokes. This may require you to correct and call out remarks and behaviors that you have ignored in the past. This may cause you to accept and even support a family member who decides to date outside of their race. We must remember that building God's kingdom is the priority, and the kingdom is for everyone! To truly dominate and multiply, we must decide to unify. This is an intentional decision made by how you live daily, and it requires your awareness and willingness to speak up.

To do this you are going to have to be liberated from the opinions of people. You are going to need a deep conviction that as a follower of Jesus, your job is to help make disciples of all nations. You are going to have to refuse to lead from your feelings and instead lead from compassion and God's heart. You will need to see people through the lens of their traumas and their experiences and bring God's truth to each situation.

CROSSING THE INVISIBLE FENCE

A few years ago I was sitting in a barbershop getting my hair cut. It was a regular day. We were all talking and laughing, when a White man with a feathered haircut walked in. He thought he was just walking in to get a haircut, but he was crossing an underlying boundary. This was "our" shop, and there was immediate tension when he walked in because of the color of his skin and the style of his hair. Shock and division paralyzed a once superrelaxed atmosphere. I felt it. We all felt it. I'm sure he felt it too.

But I also felt something else in that moment, something I'm not sure anyone else felt. I wanted to build a bridge in that moment. I'm not saying that the shock of the invisible fence disappeared, but the call to obedience, the passion that comes from being sold out, became stronger than the shock of the moment.

My neighbor's fenced-in dog had had no idea that he could gather his strength and run through the invisible barrier and find freedom on the other side. But I knew! Through moments of daily obedience to God, I had developed some shock absorption. I felt the shock, but instead of it causing me to move backward, it alerted me to act. I started a conversation with the guy in that moment and helped bridge the worlds that had collided.

This is what we are called to do! Jesus called us to love our neighbors, not put up invisible fences between our properties.

Living this life of obedience fuels passion for the kingdom and trust in God. Many times what we label as "triggers" are God's invitations for repentance and/or healing. Even as you are following Jesus beyond one fence, you might hit another. When someone says something to you that makes you want to put your invisible wall back up, or when you read a comment that brings up old feelings or fear or anger, you can take them as opportunities to heal and love outside your lines.

Our goal in life with Jesus is not to be pain-free. But because we naturally want that, our comfort can be an invisible fence. And yet following Jesus causes us to live in such a way that we can't be so comfortable that we won't confront. More times than not the person who needs the most confronting is us.

Feeling disrupted, disappointed, angry, or sad is a warning that an invisible fence is in front of you. Maybe the reason you got so frustrated with that person's comment is because you have a fence up between you and them. Maybe you've already decided that you are on the right side of the fence and they are on the wrong side of the fence no matter what. When we think that way, we'll feel ourselves getting frustrated all the time. The great thing is there is a God on the other side of it that is ready to heal you and set you free! It is in these moments that we are invited to search our hearts to find out what is really bothering us. That person who said or did that thing was probably in the wrong, but they also revealed a fence in your heart that you need to repent of. When we repent and acknowledge what was wrong about that thing, that thought, or that decision, we can start to change our thinking.

This is how you live sold out, y'all!

It is going to cost you some comfort, and it might cost you some relationships. It is a narrow path and sometimes a lonely journey. I am not going to tell you that crossing these invisible fences is a comfortable life filled with friends and people who agree with you. That's a lie! You may be called a sellout far more than you will ever be recognized as sold out. Those insults, that shade being thrown at you, might just be a little shock in your collar. It means you are getting close to an invisible boundary. You may still feel fine but those who are sending that shock are now uncomfortable. But if you want to love outside the lines, you have to keep going. You have to move forward knowing there is still a God on the other side of that fence inviting you to come over, and as you do you are giving testimony to those who are insulting you out of their own pain that they can be healed too.

YOU ARE A BRIDGE BUILDER

So what are the frustrations of today?

It depends on whose yard you are in. I sit in a painful place as a Black father in America. It's almost daily that I get another report of a child tried as an adult and labeled "aggressive" because of the color of their skin. Another injustice. Another Black man dying or attacked. I sit in spaces where I am an invited guest in the company of people who will post racially insensitive things online, where I am tolerated because I can preach, but if they had never heard of me and I was just a man walking in the door uninvited, I would not be treated as kindly.

I've been treated unjustly, I have had family members treated unjustly, and I hear the cries of the people around me, but I'm called to build a bridge. I am Ananias being told by God to pray for Saul over and over again. I am Ananias despite what the community says around me, despite what the media says around me. I must believe what God said about serving all people—that the gospel is for all people, and I am responsible for all those I come across, not just the ones who look like me. Not only do I need to seek out Saul, I must put my hands on him and call him "brother." I must live my life in a way that the Sauls of today have an opportunity to be a part of God's family.

The same is true about you. You are a bridge builder who is called to cross over boundaries and invisible lines to bring people together.

I've had several conversations with friends both Black and White who are confronted with their invisible fence when their teenage child wants to date someone outside of their race. Their hearts are often well-intentioned, and the questions of how to navigate the situation are genuine. But their questions aren't based on what they themselves think or even how to help their child navigate dating. Their questions come out of a deep concern about what their family will think. How will their child be treated by other family members?

These situations are familiar to many courageous Jesus followers who are daring to journey beyond cultural norms and the acceptable limits of family fences to build the bridges we desperately need.

Recently I got to witness a moment where a family was confronted with their fences and started dealing with them by the grace of God. I was ministering at a church that had two

Sunday services, and one of the families attending the church was divided.

When the daughter began to date a man outside of their race, she crossed a boundary that her parents were not prepared for. Their way of dealing with it was to allow the rift to deepen in their family, and they made their daughter make a choice: it was either him or them.

They were allowing their expectations to divide their family.

They were letting their opinion limit her options.

The daughter chose the guy and they got married, and the rest of the family allowed that decision to keep them divided. The parents continued going to the same church, but they always attended a different service from their daughter and her husband.

On the Sunday I visited, God impacted the parents in that first service so much that they went home, called their daughter, and began a conversation about this stronghold that was keeping their family divided. That phone call was them pushing past their invisible fence and allowing the healing to begin. I don't know where they are today, but I hope that they are continuing the journey to love outside the lines.

According to Scripture we are citizens of heaven (Philippians 3:20), meaning whatever agenda you have is secondary to the kingdom agenda, because our citizenship trumps the color of our skin. So as you continue to listen to these stories I share, I challenge you to let God impact your life the same way He impacted that family in church that Sunday. Let Him dig up any and all invisible fences in your life. Don't ignore them—address them head on.

Because this is what God wants to do in our lives. It's time to dig up any stronghold in your life that is creating an invisible fence—any strong opinions, strong points of view, or strong convictions that are counter to the commission of Christ. You may have opinions about all these things, but those opinions are secondary to the kingdom agenda. As followers of Jesus, let's stop allowing invisible fences to separate us from the kingdom work we are called to.

ARE YOU READY?

What about you, business leader? What about you, stay-at-home parent? What about you, student? What about you, Christ follower? This is going to take more than listening to a diversity message from an outside preacher on a Sunday. It is going to take more than listening to a podcast or even reading this book. This is not just a pastor's or a church leader's responsibility.

There is a reason God created you how He created you and placed you where He placed you. He created you to break down barriers and love outside the lines!

This is your job, but you must make the choice to act.

You much choose to be sold out every day.

Are you ready to look at some things you may have aligned with in the past that you now see contradict God's heart? Are you ready to face the rejection that may come?

You're critical to building God's kingdom because there are

rooms that your pastor will never be in; there are conversations that your group leader will never be a part of. You may need to have some uncomfortable conversations.

Do you know what I learned about invisible dog fences? Dogs still get out. When the excitement or fear or whatever emotion they are feeling causes them to move fast, they bypass the shock and go beyond the fence. That's when they realize the shock from their collar wasn't really debilitating. It was an annoyance and could be ignored.

The kingdom of heaven has drawn near; God is calling us to move toward unity. But only those who are sold out and brave enough to move beyond their invisible fences will achieve unity. It is those who are sold out who make that leap, because when you are sold out your win changes. It is not about staying in your safe yard anymore. It's about passing that invisible boundary and following Jesus into the uttermost.

In the coming chapters we are going to get practical and talk about how we can start to take some steps over the invisible fences in our lives and love outside the lines. Some of the steps are going to be uncomfortable, but I know you are up for it.

It's time to be sold out!

—————————— HEART CHECK ——————————

- After reading this chapter, what do you think it means to be sold out? Would you consider yourself sold out? Why or why not?

- What are some of the invisible boundaries you run into? What are some of the invisible boundaries you notice other people running into?
- What are the cultural norms that you have valued in your life over kingdom culture?

God, I pray that You would help me to identify the invisible fences and unspoken boundaries in my life—whatever has prohibited me from exploring the unfamiliar beyond my comfort zone. Help me to break free from the expectations of a few so that I may be open to greater perspective and experience the beauty and diversity of many. As I confront what I thought I knew as truth, broaden my mind that I might experience the benefits of my brothers and sisters who may not look like me. Help me to listen when my limited experience and fenced-off mindset tempt me to insist on my own viewpoint. And as I head into the rest of this book, empower me to build bridges and carry my love outside the lines!

FOUR

A DIFFERENT APPETITE

*It is the Holy Spirit who places and feeds
the hunger inside of us for unity.*

Several years ago Irene and I visited the great state of Colorado.

At the time our marriage was struggling. We were still together, but there was a massive division between us. As a last-ditch effort to save our marriage, we went to this small town in the middle of Colorado to spend some time with a counselor. The town only had one traffic light and not a single other Black person I could see. I seemed to be the only Black guy around, and since Irene is biracial, I had a fear that if something went down, her White side would take over, and she'd probably side with everyone else. Not really, she would never do that; that was just my paranoia of sticking out like a sore thumb.

One evening we were hungry after a long day of counseling, so we walked into a local restaurant and were met by a whole lot of stares. As we walked to our table, I felt like a fish out of water; everyone was watching. The worst stares were coming from a large table in the back. It was a party of eight, and the guy at the very end of the table was looking right at me.

His stare caused me to create a narrative in my head that he wasn't happy I was there. I don't know if he had a problem or if I was just being paranoid, but in my mind, he had a line drawn and I was on the wrong side of it.

As we enjoyed our meal, I felt the gaze of the people in the room, and every time I glanced over at the table, the guy at the end was staring me down. But I also felt something else; I felt the Holy Spirit tell me to pay for that table of eight. That's right: pay, not pray.

Really? I prayed, trying to wrestle and bargain with the Holy Spirit. *Don't you see that table with two White people over there? How about I pay for them?* But God wanted me to pay for all eight of them, because He wanted this to cost me something.

When the waiter came over, I pointed to the table full of angry stares and said, "I'd like to cover their meal."

"Really?" she said in response. "Are you sure?"

"Yeah, I'm sure."

She went back and told the rest of the staff what was going on, and then she went over and told the table of eight. Everyone in the restaurant was watching at this point.

When they got up to leave, I made eye contact with the man who had been staring at me all evening. I walked over and stuck out my hand. I suspected it was the first time he had ever been near a Black person. I assumed he had a wall up, a fence, and as I reached across that invisible line and shook his hand, the wall fell. The fact that I shook up his potential stereotype inspired him to shake my hand. Truly, I felt his entire countenance change, from judgment and discomfort to relaxation and acceptance.

Something happened to me in that moment. I walked into that restaurant because I was hungry for some good food, but I walked out with a different kind of hunger. I took a risk, loving outside the lines, and although it cost me something, it also brought down the walls in the room that were keeping us separated from one another. As Irene and I got in the car and drove away, I realized God was giving me a new appetite. I was hungry to love over more lines and experience more unity.

GO THROUGH SAMARIA

I sometimes wonder what the disciples were thinking when they said yes to following Jesus. Today we have the New Testament to let us know what we are getting ourselves into, but they did not have that. What did they have to go on? Jesus was already presenting differently than the Jews expected Messiah to come. He was born of parents who were not of a priestly tribe, raised in Galilee, and was essentially homeless. There were no fact-checkers and no blue check to verify His social identity. Without the knowledge of the gospel that you have today, would you follow this man? Yet the disciples did, and He took them through many life-changing experiences.

One of the most critical detours Jesus called His disciples to make on their journey was through Samaria to have a conversation with an unsuspecting woman at a well.

In John 4 we read about Jesus making a trip from the Judean countryside back to His hometown of Galilee. The most direct way to make the trip was to go through Samaria, but there was an issue. Jews and Samaritans did not get along. The tension between the two was so bad that if a Jew came into contact with a Samaritan, they would have to go to the temple to cleanse themselves before they were permitted to reenter society.

Jews making the journey from Judea to Galilee would travel seventy miles out of the way just to avoid Samaria. This had become their way of life; there was no questioning it, and there was no room for negotiation. Jews and Samaritans did not mix. Jesus was setting them up to go into the part of town where they were not welcome and where the negative feeling was mutual. A hard line had been drawn, a division that dated back for many years, and there was no hope for reconciliation. They just decided to be apart and stay apart.

But Jesus told His disciples, a group of Jewish men, that they needed to go through Samaria this time. I love how the Bible doesn't mention any resistance from the disciples, which makes me wonder what they thought about this: *What do You mean we have to go through Samaria? Because we actually don't have to go through Samaria. No one, no Jew, goes through Samaria, so why do we have to?*

This was not an optional invitation for them, and it isn't for us either. Jesus was about to carry His love outside the lines and go to Samaria to have a life-altering conversation with a woman who needed it. As followers of Christ we are to do the same.

The Messiah did not come for just a select few; He did not come just for people who looked like Him, grew up like Him, or spoke His language. Jesus came for all, and the disciples had a front-row seat to that.

This earth is not our home; we are on a journey to our heavenly residence, and there are some stops we must make along the way. There is no going around it—we need to go through it. If we are called, if we are truly living out the Great Commission to make disciples of all nations, then that means we must go where all people are and not just some people.

WHAT'S YOUR SAMARIA?

What is Samaria for us today? In our culture "Samaria" might be the part of town we avoid. Or the Samaritan might be the person who causes us to quietly lock our car doors when we see them approaching. We avoid and we lock; we stay comfortable. But as followers of Jesus we cannot avoid this anymore. It's time to go through Samaria, to start having conversations with people who don't look like us, and to wrestle with the parts of us that are resistant to this.

I get it: no one wants to go to Samaria. It's uncertain, inconvenient, and uncomfortable. But we cannot sweep these uncomfortable conversations or situations under the rug any longer. We must go through Samaria because Jesus did, and we cannot call ourselves disciples of Jesus without the willingness to follow Him where He goes.

THE WOMAN AT THE WELL

Once Jesus and the disciples reached Samaria, they stopped at a place called Sychar to take a break. They were weary from travel and needed to be refreshed, so the disciples went to look for food and Jesus stayed behind at a well to rest. This wasn't just any well; it was Jacob's well. Jacob was a descendent of Abraham, the man we talked about in chapter 1 who originally heard God's call to carry love outside the lines.

But thousands of years later, God's people were still drawing lines around this town.

While Jesus was sitting there, a Samaritan woman walked up to the well to get water. It was the hottest part of the day, which was not the time most people go get water, so there was a good chance this woman was braving the heat of the day because she was an outcast in her community. We find out in the story that she'd had five husbands. We don't know why that was, but it's easy to stereotype, isn't it? It's easy to jump to conclusions and assume it's because she was doing something wrong. And apparently the rest of the town was doing the same thing, because she was ostracized and undesirable to her own Samaritan community, and so she had to brave the heat of the day on her own.

Because that's what division does, right? It leaves us to brave the heat on our own. Between all the racism, classism, and ageism in our nation (and our world) today, the heat is being turned up. And the hotter it gets, the more divided we become. Many people I talk to resonate with this woman—they feel like they are being left to brave the heat of our culture on their own.

This woman was used to people drawing lines and excluding her from the party. And when she saw Jesus, a Jewish man, sitting at the well, she probably assumed the same old thing was going to happen all over again.

Jesus began the conversation by asking her for something to drink. She was not used to anyone asking her for water, let alone a Jewish man, and it surprised her and threw her off so much that she started her response with, "You Jews . . ."

You can see the racist, classist, and sexist barriers just in the way she responded to Him. If there was ever a phrase guaranteed to push people away, it's "You people." You Black people. You White people. You poor people. You rich people.

It sounds as though her speech may have been seasoned with a hint of hate, a bit of distrust, and a lot of prejudice.

She was putting Him in His place, classifying Him as not one of her own. We do the same thing today. Classism (prejudice for or against people belonging to a particular social class) is real, and it's one of the major ways we draw lines and place people outside our in-group.

I experience this every time I go to the airport. People stop me and say, "Hey, are you an athlete? You are so big, what team do you play for?" I've heard that comment so many times, and it's never once been from another Black person. I watch Irene deal with these comments too. As soon as she starts talking, people will be so intrigued and say things like, "You talk so proper" or "Look at your hair. How do you do that with your hair?"

All these comments are people trying to put us in a social class. In boxes. In carefully drawn lines.

But it's not time to put people in classes; it's time to start going to class and learning what it really means to follow Jesus. We all need to be educated in loving outside the lines and outside classism, and Jesus taught a master class. He knew exactly what this woman was doing, and instead of approaching her about her lack He began the conversation with what she had to give.

Even in the face of tension and deep-rooted prejudice, He dignified her. She was a Samaritan, He was a Jew; she was a woman, He was a man; she was in sin, He did not sin. They were as different as different could be, and He started the conversation with a statement that showed that she had value to give.

The dictionary defines dignity as "the state or quality of being worthy of honor or respect."[1] This is where we begin. Dishonor and disrespect divide us, but dignity puts us on the path to unity. You cannot have true diversity if you do not start with dignity.

Desegregation didn't begin in Maryland until the mid-1960s. My father grew up having to drink from a water fountain that was labeled "Colored Only." There were laws created to keep us "separate but equal," all meant to keep Black people in a subservient role to White people. To strip them of dignity and keep them separate.

We are many years away from that, and yes, the physical signs to keep us separate have been removed, but the impact remains. We still live with unspoken rules of what we can and cannot do with certain people because of our biases and stereotypes.

This is what Jesus addressed when He asked the Samaritan woman for water. He saw her as one of His own, and He dignified her.

Dignity is valuing a person, looking at them as having something to offer. I was recently discussing diversity with someone and they shared with me a list of their outreach initiatives. Dignity and diversity are not outreach initiatives! If I am asking you about your interactions with people who do not look like you and your first or only response to me is how you have helped the disenfranchised, then we have work to do.

You do realize people of color are not just poor and don't just live in the inner city, right? You know they are millionaires, doctors, lawyers, judges, CEOs, and philanthropists, right? You know they live in the suburbs, the country, and penthouses, not just in the ghetto, right?

We must uproot these biases that have been around for years, go a different way, and talk to different people. It's possible to have meaningful relationships with people who don't look like us, but those friendships must start with valuing one another. People aren't problems to fix; they are human beings who deserve our love and respect. We must open the conversation with dignity and maintain that as we listen to one another.

Do not reduce your diversity to service—or under the spiritual umbrella of "ministering to the poor"—as this does not pull up the roots of racism now disguised as classism. It is easy to pass out food, but Jesus had dinner with all kinds of people. It is easy to pass out a water bottle, but Jesus asked for a drink. Throughout His conversation with the Samaritan woman, Jesus engaged without condemnation, without trying to drive a point home. He maintained that dignity all the way through, even while speaking some tough truths.

WHY ARE YOU TALKING TO HER?

After all this happened the disciples arrived back at the well. Remember, they had gone off to find a Popeyes and get a chicken sandwich, but when they returned, they were shocked that Jesus was talking to the Samaritan woman. That's a perfect picture of the tension that the disciples (and all of us, if we are being honest) faced. Jesus came to earth to love outside the lines, but His disciples always wanted to stay inside the lines. Jesus wanted to visit the ends of the earth, but the disciples wanted to stay in their comfort zone. Jesus wanted to bridge the gap, but the disciples wanted to widen the gap. Jesus wanted to be the church for anyone and everyone, but the disciples just wanted to go to church with the people who looked just like them, voted like them, and behaved like them.

So when they asked Jesus why He was talking to the woman, His response was key: "My food . . . is to do the will of him who sent me" (John 4:34).

Did you catch that? Jesus had a different appetite!

His appetite was to do the will of His Father and live and love outside the lines! The disciples didn't understand that yet—their appetite wasn't ready to change—but they kept showing up and trusting Jesus. And later on in the story, once the Holy Spirit arrived, they began to develop this new appetite as well.

THERE IS HELP

Living and loving outside the lines can be difficult, and let me tell you, I get frustrated from time to time. I am pained when I see people neglect Samaria. I am pained to go to church after church and still see the segregation. I am pained to still hear of believers approaching conversations with more passion to make a point than they are to listen. But the thing that keeps me going and gives me strength from day to day is the Holy Spirit.

It is the Holy Spirit who gives us a different appetite, who allows us to be restored and refreshed by conversations that lovingly lead people to God. It is the Holy Spirit who places and feeds the hunger inside of us for unity.

Acts 2:17 says, "I will pour out my Spirit on all people." That means everybody. The Holy Spirit is no respecter of gender, age, race, or class. When the Holy Spirit is poured out, walls of division are erased.

When Jesus talked to the woman at Jacob's well, He told her, "Whoever drinks the water I give them will never thirst. Indeed, the water I give them will become in them a spring of water welling up to eternal life" (John 4:14). The woman thought this conversation was about actual water, but Jesus was talking about the Holy Spirit.

The Holy Spirit is the intermediary between divided parties, the one who could bring Jews and Samaritans back together. Our job is to start with dignity, and then the Holy Spirit steps in and transforms our dignity into diversity and ultimately into unity.

The same thing is true for us today—the Holy Spirit is ready to step in and transform lives.

What is the Holy Spirit saying to you right now? Where is the well, the meeting place for you and someone who does not look like you, someone who is of another culture or of another race? That restaurant in Colorado was a well for me. My wife and I looked different from everyone else there, and in that moment, the Holy Spirit taught me that loving outside the lines was going to cost me something over and over again. Yeah, I could have paid for the table of two or just ignored the holy prompting all together. But I couldn't, because I would be denying my own calling and denying the power of the Holy Spirit at work in me.

Do you currently have any wells in your life? Any places you are spending time at where most people don't look like you? If not, maybe it's time to add some detours to your life—to find a Samaria. And when you see lines clearly being drawn, ask the Holy Spirit to give you compassion, empathy, and a resolve to do better.

How do you react when you learn of racial injustice? What came up for you when you heard reports of the Charleston church shooting? What did you think or feel when you watched the reporting of the trials of the men who killed Ahmaud Arbery or George Floyd on your favorite news channel? Did you see Arbery and Floyd as your brothers?

It didn't matter to Jesus that the woman at the well was from Samaria. It mattered that she was hurt; it mattered that she needed a friend. Jesus met her where she was. Do people get that from you?

Jesus met this woman and talked to her; He dignified her. That dignity gave her the ability to ask questions in return. When He spoke about giving her water, she remarked that He had no bucket to draw with and no rope to pull with. She questioned His ability to meet the need that He intended to fill. She was right in the physical sense—He could not give her water. He didn't have a bucket or a rope. Wanting to give her a drink was not enough without the right tools.

It is the same with us. The woman stands at the well and asks of us today: Do you have a bucket—a capacity to love humanity? Do you have a rope—are you committed to this? It is going to take more than wanting racial reconciliation. You must have the heart and the commitment to live it out.

We must have the capacity to listen to hurts without getting defensive or making it about ourselves. We must have the commitment to talk and build lasting relationships, not just when there is breaking news or another riot or protest. I'm so thankful I have White friends who don't just check in with me when there is another heartbreaking event, but who care enough about me to see how I'm doing all the time. I try to be the same type of friend for them, because wanting to be friends is not enough—we actually have to take the steps to become friends. We have to bear one another's burdens. We have to live this out.

YOUR UTTERMOST

The power of the Holy Spirit is not about a feeling or emotion; it is about growth. It is about being a witness. Jesus clarified the purpose of the Holy Spirit in Acts 1:8 when He said, "But ye shall receive power, after that the Holy Ghost is come upon you: and ye shall be witnesses unto me both in Jerusalem, and in all Judaea, and in Samaria, and unto the uttermost part of the earth" (KJV). He reinforced Samaria in that reference. He told His disciples that they would be a witness to those nearest to them and to those they were taught not to like.

He went even further than that when He said "the uttermost." That word is *eschatos*, meaning "time, space, and rank."[2] There is something beyond Samaria that we are called to reach, something we cannot do on our own. We cannot witness Jesus Christ beyond our time, space, and rank. Who are the people you spend the least amount of time with? That is your uttermost. Who are the people farthest from you? That is your uttermost. Who are the very last people on your list? They are your uttermost. You have been given the Holy Spirit to do just that, to reach your uttermost.

But it's not easy. Our preference is to stay in our comfort zone.

I'll never forget the first time Irene and I went out to buy a new couch together. I'm six feet three and weigh two hundred pounds and some change (a lot of change), and she's only five feet four. Obviously she would prefer to buy a couch that fits her perfectly, but that couch isn't going to work for me. The one we landed on was outside her comfort zone; her feet don't even come close to touching the ground. She had to be okay with sitting and watching TV outside of her comfort zone so that we could get a couch that worked for me. But she sacrificed her comfort so that we can be together.

It's uncomfortable to be in a place where you care less about your own time, space, and rank in this world. It takes time to build relationship, it takes space in our lives to listen to experiences we know nothing about and respond with empathy, and it may cost you your "rank" in your social circle. This is impossible to do without the work of the Holy Spirit inside of you—and how do you strengthen that? You feed it.

This is what Jesus was talking about when He said, "My food . . . is to do the will of him who sent me" (John 4:34). When we continue to obey the promptings of the Holy Spirit, we feed the appetite of being Spirit-led. We start to develop a palate for what pleases God's heart.

A NEW PALATE

When I was younger, I hated blue cheese. The smell of it, the look of it, it was all wrong. And I don't think I'm alone in that. Blue cheese is fungus. Who would ever want to eat fungus? Whenever we would go out to eat and one of my parents ordered blue cheese dressing, I would turn up my nose at it. I did not even want to look at it. I didn't understand how people could stand the stuff; it was moldy cheese!

Not too long ago I was at an event and a wedge salad was placed in front of me. I was pretty absorbed in conversation at the table, so I wasn't paying much attention at first to the salad. As I began to eat, my focus shifted—this was the best salad I'd ever had in my life! I began to rave about it, and I had to ask the waiter, "What dressing is this? I love it!" Imagine my shock when the response was, "It's blue cheese dressing."

Blue cheese?

Really?

I couldn't believe it. I had spent the greater part of my life hating blue cheese and refusing to go near it.

I started to wonder what other things I had missed out on. I had never stopped to think about that: With all the change that had taken place in my life as I had grown, had my palate changed too?

Yes!

Things my parents loved, like chicken livers, were gross to me as a kid, and now I love them. I was glad to have this awakening to show me what I was missing and give me a different appetite that set me up to desire things I had not before.

Experiences help our palates change. The woman at the well hated Jews and her fellow Samaritans, but after experiencing the love of Jesus, she learned to love them, too, because experiences help our palates change. Love is the intermediary, the thing that brings us together. And it's only through experiencing the Holy

Spirit that we can begin to love what we used to hate, celebrate what we used to tolerate, and embrace what we used to prohibit. Love is the thing that moves us outside our lines.

Obeying the Holy Spirit by doing things like paying for eight people to eat diner food or listening to understand instead of trying to make a point develops our palates. We start to enjoy it and we realize we may have been missing out on things.

Friends, we need to grow up. We need to develop a different appetite. We need to have an appetite to see how God sees. We need an appetite to hear what God hears. We need an appetite to reach out to our uttermost and bring them in as family. We cannot continue to avoid Samaria. We cannot continue to only consider racial injustice when something horrific—like the killings of Trayvon Martin, Michael Brown, or George Floyd—crosses our news feed. We must live it.

In order to reach where no one is reaching, you have to go where no one will go. You have to be able to go there in conversations filled with dignity and led by the Holy Spirit. So are you ready? Are you ready to have your appetite changed?

The disciples were uncomfortable with Samaria at first; they didn't understand why Jesus would lead them across that line. But later, by the book of Acts, those same disciples had developed a palate not just for Samaria but for the ends of the earth. Like eating blue cheese, learning to love outside the lines is an acquired taste—it might be a little uncomfortable at first, but before you know it, you'll learn to love it, and you'll realize you've developed a whole new appetite.

—————————— HEART CHECK ——————————

- What is your response after reading this chapter? How do you find yourself taking sides rather than seeking to understand different experiences?
- What is your Samaria, your uttermost? Who or what is a person, place, or problem in the area of race relations that you have been avoiding? Why do you think you've been avoiding it and what would it look like to address it?
- Have you noticed yourself developing a new appetite for working toward unity? What actionable things can you do to bring life, healing, and satisfaction to yourself?

Father, give me the desire to reach people no one is reaching and the courage to go to the places where others refuse to. Show me the places and people that following Jesus requires me to visit. Help me to live so that no one ever feels ostracized, overlooked, or outcast by anything I do or say. Lead me to have a heart of compassion and seek conversation and comradery. Help me to be sensitive and

receptive to the prompting of the Holy Spirit to celebrate people who are different from me rather than avoiding or tolerating our differences. Make me more like Jesus so that my uncompromising compassion allows me to be a witness to not only those who are close but also those who are currently far from me. Give me an appetite to do only the will of God who sent me no matter who He sends me to.

FIVE

GOD'S GUMBO

God wants one kingdom: one pot, with
each ingredient, each person, playing
their part in the flavor profile!

There's nothing like a good ol' pot of gumbo.

When it's time for me to make my gumbo for family and friends, I go big. Because gumbo is meant to be shared—it's meant to be enjoyed together. It's one of my signature dishes, and you need to understand I take pride in the beauty that is my gumbo. I will plan around making it because I want to take my time with the process and savor all the components.

The first thing I do is gather all the different ingredients— green peppers, red peppers, celery, smoked sausage, and a long list of other things. Then I grab the giant wooden spoon I got from Zambia. Irene's mother was Zambian, and she showed me how to cook with this spoon.

I love the fact that the dish I am known for was born out of diversity. Gumbo is a dish popular in Louisiana and was created by the different cultures that were mixed in that area. It has African, Spanish, French, and Native American influences in its culinary process. Maybe that is why gumbo is so good! The basis of gumbo itself is taking many different things that are good on their own and bringing them together to make something delicious.

Any gumbo begins with something chefs call the "holy trinity," a mix of onion, celery, and green pepper. Separately those three ingredients are not as awesome as they can be together. These three very strong components need a base and time. This base is called a *roux*. The roux is a mix of fat and flour, and it adds richness and depth, providing a base for all the ingredients to meld together to become a gumbo. Without the roux, it's not gumbo; it's just soup.

If only humans were as malleable as the ingredients of gumbo. This one pot of deliciousness is made up of so many different ingredients, and the magic is in the blending of flavors in the roux while they still hold their distinction. If only we could understand that unity is not uniformity. We can unite and come together while still holding our distinctions, for unity is not a bunch of the same thing coming together for one purpose but different things coming together for one purpose. God wants us to come together for one glorious purpose. As good as my gumbo is, what God wants to bring together in all of us is infinitely better.

I can't imagine cooking a pot of gumbo and having only

shrimp, or only crab, or only chicken, or only vegetables—that is not gumbo; that's just shrimp soup, crab soup, chicken soup, or vegetable soup. To achieve the distinction of an elevated gumbo, all these proteins and all these vegetables must come together with the rich base of a roux. They all have to play their part in the flavor profile; it is the only way to be gumbo.

GOD'S DESIGN

God designed His kingdom to work a lot like gumbo. He created each one of us to be a unique ingredient that comes together to form something even more delicious. This design is laid out for us on the very first page of Scripture: "Then God said, 'Let Us make man in Our image, according to Our likeness; let them have dominion over the fish of the sea, over the birds of the air, and over the cattle, over all the earth and over every creeping thing that creeps on the earth'" (Genesis 1:26 NKJV).

Notice God said, "Let Us make man in Our image," not "Let Me make man in My image." It's plural because God exists as a Holy Trinity. God is one essence but three persons—Father, Son, and Holy Spirit.

Think about the fact that you and I are made in the image of this triune God. Think about how multifaceted this creation is. Think about how diverse people are. And now consider that each one of us is a unique image of this God. That's another reason why diversity is so important—it helps us realize that God is even bigger and more expansive than we could ever comprehend.

Just like any good pot of gumbo, God has a lot of flavor and God has a lot of color.

God created us to be fruitful, multiply, and have dominion. We are made to rule, to have authority, and to have dominion in His kingdom. God created us to rule over creation—the birds of the air and the fish of the sea. But notice He never gave us a command to rule over one another.

Drawing lines and ruling over one another was our idea, not God's idea. And all those lines keep us from coming together in the way God created us to. Instead of being God's gumbo, we end up staying apart as separate ingredients sitting on the kitchen counter. The lines between us are keeping us from experiencing our full potential. We are staying separate instead of coming together to form something delicious.

God's kingdom was originally created to be fruitful. It was the kingdom that healed, and it was the kingdom that gathered diverse people together. God's kingdom is not a divided one; His fruit is unity and not division. As carriers of the kingdom of heaven, we should be doing the same thing. Our lives should be marked by diversity and unity.

God doesn't want a White kingdom, a Black kingdom, a Latino kingdom, or an Asian kingdom. He wants one kingdom: one pot, with each ingredient, each person, playing their part in the flavor profile.

It's kind of like walking down the toothpaste aisle at the grocery store. Some whiten your teeth and others prevent cavities. Some help protect sensitive teeth and others taste like bubblegum. But let's be real—they all do the same thing. It's all toothpaste. It's just packaged in lots of different ways. I'm so glad we have lots of different options. When I walk down the aisle with Irene, we end up picking out two different tubes. And when our kids were young and didn't want to brush their teeth, we were thankful for the bubblegum toothpaste. When it comes to toothpaste, I'm grateful for diversity.

God's kingdom is a lot like the toothpaste aisle. Although we are all trying to accomplish the same thing, we are meant to bring our own flavor to the table.

What does this mean for us?

If we want to be God's gumbo, we must check our hearts in our serving.

Am I serving a group of people to check off a spiritual box, or am I willing to enter someone's world and break bread with them like Jesus did? It means a heart check in our relationships. Am I only comfortable with people who look like me? If so, why is that?

The goal in cross-cultural relationships is not to always be comfortable. Instead we're called to confront the uneasiness in our hearts and minds when we are around a people and cultures unfamiliar to us. We must really sit and ask ourselves some tough questions. *Am I making disciples? Do those I am discipling bear the fruit of Christ? Does my area of dominion show God's love, His unity, His heart? Am I reaching out beyond who and what I am comfortable with so that I'm dealing with who and what make me feel uncomfortable?*

Those aren't easy questions to ask, but they are important questions to answer. God's kingdom is identified by its fruit, by how we live. And if we want to bear fruit, we must be willing to ask the right questions and dig up the roots of racism.

SALT AND LIGHT

In Matthew 5, Jesus stood on a mountainside with His disciples and captured the attention of a diverse crowd who had been following Him. The message He shared with them was extremely important. So important that it's worth reading a large portion of it together. Don't skip over this passage. Listen to Jesus' words as if He is talking to you, because He is.

> Let me tell you why you are here. You're here to be salt-seasoning that brings out the God-flavors of this earth. If you lose your saltiness, how will people taste godliness? You've lost your usefulness and will end up in the garbage.
>
> Here's another way to put it: You're here to be light, bringing out the God-colors in the world. God is not a secret to be kept. We're going public with this, as public as a city on a hill. If I make you light-bearers, you don't think I'm going to hide you under a bucket, do you? I'm putting you on a light stand. Now that I've put you there on a hilltop, on a light stand—shine! Keep open house; be generous with your lives. By opening up to others, you'll prompt people to open up with God, this generous Father in heaven. (Matthew 5:13–16 MSG)

God calls us to be salt and light. He calls us to be influential. Kingdom influence is not preferential; it is all-inclusive. This is where we live beyond ourselves and love beyond our preferences. Kingdom influence means we can add our personal, cultural flavor no matter what environment we are in. We add to the flavor no matter what pot we are in. We were designed in such a way that although we are meant to be with others, we do not lose ourselves.

Have you ever bitten into a raw onion? Nasty, right?

The true power of the onion is evoked when it is cut and cooked to add to the flavor of other ingredients. On its own it is nowhere near as great as it is lending its strength to other ingredients that may look, smell, or taste nothing like it. But when you cut the onion and add it to the roux as part of the holy trinity with green peppers and celery, you have something so much deeper, better, and pleasing. That original onion is not lost at all; if anything, its flavor is enhanced by its collaboration.

Salt is also necessary because a little bit of salt awakens everything that is present but lying dormant. Salt enhances—it brings other things to the surface. Salt influences. Salt has the capacity to be a powerful and compelling force, to make the ordinary extraordinary. It can change and affect anything it is paired with. It enhances flavor. Without salt many foods are bland and tasteless. We are God's flavors and colors. Which is why Jesus calls us to be the salt of the earth.

Different people—God colors.

Different cultures—God flavors.

I love that Jesus referenced salt in speaking of our purpose. He literally said that our value is determined by the value we bring out of others. Not in what we have, not in what we look like, not even in how we worship Him, but in how we treat others. And in how we treat others that are not like us.

Being in relationships with those who are different from us is the first step. Unity is the next step. In order to get to this next step, we must value one another. We must value what makes us different. We must value one another's experiences. We must value the work that God is doing in the person across the room or across the globe.

We must be salt and light.

SALT SUBSTITUTES

Several years ago I went on a golf trip with a bunch of guys, and I wanted to make gumbo for the group. A few of them went to the store to get the ingredients, and someone bought a salt substitute.

Now usually I would have spotted this, but I was so busy cooking and hanging out with the fellas that I didn't even notice. But when we sat down to eat, it was horrible! The salt substitute ruined the entire dish and we ended up throwing it away.

This knock-off salt gave the appearance that it was going to bring out the flavors. The packaging was similar, the look and smell was similar, but when it was time to do what salt did, it did the opposite. It made the gumbo taste worse. You could taste the offensive fake salt overpowering the other ingredients. It was useless and destroyed the whole pot.

What about you? Are there any areas in which you have been a salt substitute? Have you appeared to care but just didn't? Have you tried to overpower someone's experience with your opinion? Instead of seeking to understand, have you simply tried to interpret others' experiences with your limited mindset? Have you lost your value because you failed to bring out the value in others? Have you minimized your true kingdom influence to be salt? Have you ruined the taste of the kingdom for others because you were a salt substitute? If you still have breath in your lungs, then you still have time to change that. Don't be a salt substitute, leaving a nasty aftertaste or experience of who God is. Find places where you can be salt.

How can you be salt at your kid's soccer game when all the parents have chosen seats in the bleachers that cause them to be segregated? How can you invite the person who is sitting alone at the party or in the cafeteria at school? And when you notice value in another person at work, how can you call that potential out of them and celebrate it in front of other employees? How can you throw others into the pot and bring out their value?

Diversity is not just inclusion; diversity is appreciating what makes us different. In gumbo there are no wasted pieces. I can throw in a jalapeño if I want to. The salt, the roux, all these things work together to make something rich and distinct.

This is God's kingdom. When we are the salt, we enhance the value of others.

The first chef I ever watched prepare gumbo was Emeril

Lagasse. He's the person I heard refer to onion, celery, and green pepper as the holy trinity. My favorite part about watching Emeril cook is when he adds salt, he'll shout, "*Bam!*"

You can feel the excitement in his voice because he knows the spice is about to make the whole dish better.

I wonder what would happen if we started getting that excited about being the salt that is added into situations, because we know when we get added to the pot, we are going to make everyone better.

When there is disunity, "*Bam!*"

When there is friction, "*Bam!*"

When people are trying to draw lines and exclude others, "*Bam!*"

Jesus calls us to be salt, and there is nothing worse than preparing a dish with a salt substitute. Be the ingredient God created you to be. Because when that ingredient gets added to the gumbo, it makes the gumbo that much better.

"*Bam!*" Let's step up and be the salt!

CAN YOU SEE ME?

When I was younger I entered a singing competition.

Nervous doesn't begin to describe what I felt during the long wait for my turn to sing. I remember standing there fidgeting and inwardly coaching myself, waiting for my name to be called. Finally the emcee called my name; I got up on that stage, and I did the best I could.

Now, I heard the applause, but I couldn't fully embrace that moment because my mind was still on the road ahead. I had to come back down from that stage into another long waiting period filled with anxious thoughts while everyone else took their turn. After what felt like hours, the final results came in, and I had lost. I was pretty confident that I'd been at least among the top three contestants, but I wasn't. Filled with disappointment, I asked one of the judges what I could have done better.

"We couldn't see your eyes," he stated. "I couldn't see you."

I wasn't wearing a hat pulled down low. I wasn't wearing a big hoody. So I went away more confused than ever. But it wasn't about my headwear. I realized that the stage was poorly lit. And in a room full of contestants of lighter and darker hues, my dark skin wasn't easily seen.

I felt punished.

I felt judged by what I could not control.

If I'm being honest, I got defensive. I was the only Black person there, and I started wondering if they were being racist, if they didn't like Black people. I was really upset. I don't know their hearts, but I do at least know they weren't taking steps to see me.

In the end the reason why I lost was due to the atmosphere in the room. Those words still ring true for many today: *"I couldn't see you."*

If there is one question that can begin the journey to unity, it is this: Can you see me? Can you see me, or do you see what you have heard about people like me? Can you see me, or are you distracted by your assumptions? Can you see me, or are you blinded by what you expect me to look like and how you want me to act?

Can you see me for how unique I am? Can you see how I might be different from you, or am I lost in the mix? Will you change the lighting in your heart to acknowledge the gift that is in the room with you? Are you willing to move your seat and adjust lighting and sound controls in order to get the full experience of those around you? This is what Jesus invites us into when He calls us the light of the world. Can you see your neighbor?

We are all different. Even identical twins have differences. Our differences are the expressions of the boundless creativity of our Maker. When God made man and woman, He didn't make one type of human. He made us into different sizes, shapes, and colors. If we accept differences between members of our family bonded by blood, why don't we accept the same when we walk outside our doors?

What if someone looked through the lineup and tweaked the stage lighting because a dark-skinned boy was fifth in line? What if someone had thought to put a ramp onto the stage because kid number 53 used a wheelchair? You don't have to tell someone that you see them; your actions and reactions will speak louder than words. If you hear of another beating or murder of a Black person and you genuinely wonder how your Black friend is feeling in that moment and you call them, not just to check it off your list but because you genuinely want to hear how they are doing, that is seeing someone. Don't tell me you can see me— your acknowledgment will let me know. I will know if I am seen by your actions and reactions.

Do you see me? Do you see your daughter? Do you see your coworker? Do you see the mailman? Do you see the waiter? Do you see the bus driver? Do you see the individuality of the people you come across every day? Can you really see them? It is time to turn on the light so you can see and not just look.

For those who are resigned to isolation because you have never experienced true acceptance or even acknowledgment, I encourage you to come on stage again. We can't wait to hear you sing. We will all aim to do better to adjust the lights, sound, or whatever is needed so that we see you for everything unique that you are.

The brilliance of gumbo is that it's not about one ingredient over any other; it's about the uniqueness of each ingredient and the deliciousness that we experience when they all come together.

God's gumbo is supposed to work the same way. When every color works together, it creates something bigger and more beautiful than anything any one of us could comprehend on our own. But in order to see it, appreciate it, and practice it, we have to be willing to see one another. We have to adjust the lights and celebrate each person for the unique color and flavor they bring to the pot.

SEEING COLOR

I recently made a trip to Best Buy because I was looking for a new television.

I love watching sports; it's an experience for me. But you can't have the right experience with the wrong television. You must be able to hear everything as if you are in the arena and see everything as clearly as sitting courtside. My mission at Best Buy was to find the TV that would give me that experience.

I didn't walk into Best Buy and ask for the gray televisions. I didn't search for the aisle with the black-and-white ones. No, I asked for the highest definition possible because the more color we see, the more experience we can have. We want the 4K or 8K if they've got it; we want to see each and every color, because color is beautiful.

You would never walk into the store and ask to see things in black and white, so let's make sure we aren't doing that in life either. God has created so many different colors; let's learn to appreciate every single one.

When I'm in a conversation about race, I'll often have people tell me they are color-blind. "Oh, I didn't even notice I said that or did that because I don't see color." As if that's a convenient excuse to stop talking about it.

"I'm not," I tell them. "I see color." Because ignoring that I'm Black is ignoring the way God created me. It's missing the image of God. The starting point for loving outside the lines is not ignoring color; it's acknowledging and celebrating it because every color is precious in God's sight.

Let's learn to see one another in high definition and high diversity.

THE POWER OF UNITY

Have you ever read something in the Bible and then just immediately read it again because you felt like it was crazy? That is how I feel every time I read the story of the Tower of Babel in Genesis.

It's a semi-random story where a diverse group of people came together and started working toward a common goal, and then God confused their languages to make it more difficult.

At first glance it may sound cruel of God, or you may be tempted to blame the division on Him. But it wasn't the people coming together that brought on this response; it was their reason. The power of unity was present at the Tower of Babel—God recognized that—but the problem was they were after the wrong thing. In Genesis 11:4 we learn their motive: "Come, let us build ourselves a city, with a tower that reaches to the heavens, so that we may make a name for ourselves." They weren't coming together to make God's name great; they were coming together to make their names great.

Several generations later there was another moment where a diverse group of people came together, but this gathering had a very different outcome.

In Acts 2 all the believers came together for one reason: they had all followed Jesus. Jesus had just ascended into heaven and their following led them to one place. The Bible calls it the upper room. It was in that moment, when the followers of Jesus came together to worship and handle kingdom business, that God redeemed the separation of people. This time when God came down to visit His people He gave them the Holy Spirit, the Promised One.

That day also happened to be the day of Pentecost. So while all the followers of Jesus were in the upper room worshiping, Jerusalem was packed full of people from all around the world who all spoke different languages.

Genesis 11 is a story about God scattering people, but Acts 2 is a story about God gathering people. This time, instead of God confusing their languages, He empowered them to preach the gospel in lots of different languages, so that everyone could come together and understand who Jesus was. Here we have people gathered again, all from different parts of the known world at the time, and this time God united them and they came together as one to form God's gumbo.

What was the difference?

At the Tower of Babel, the people wanted to *be* God; in the upper room the people wanted to be *with* God. And this is the posture of heart that is needed to bring us together. Each one of them spoke in their own language—they kept their identities—but they were understood. Different cultures with one understanding, different languages with one message—they were declaring the mighty works of God. The Holy Spirit is the roux of God's gumbo, adding the richness, the depth, and bringing us all together. The Holy Spirit satisfies a holy hunger to see heaven on earth.

Two gatherings and two very different outcomes.

Diversity is a step, not our goal; our goal as believers in Jesus Christ is unity. We do not skip over diversity, and we do not stop at it either. You might feel like you have a diverse community because you have representation in the room, but until there is value you will not have unity.

If you look around, our world is extremely diverse, kind of like gumbo. But in the church, we have failed to reflect this beautiful diversity and unity. We are not living out the influence and illumination that Jesus commanded. We are missing our holy trinity. More ingredients result in a more delicious flavor, but only if they come together. The more people, the more opportunity for God flavors, but only if we step over the lines and boundaries we've created and come together. Our different skin tones are God colors and God flavors.

Simply put, we are better together.

What happened in the upper room is a picture of a cry of hunger by a diverse and unified group reaching toward heaven in a way that got God's attention and put into motion God's plan to unite us again through His Spirit. It is the Holy Spirit that gives all believers the power to be a witness, the power to see others and bring out their value. The Holy Spirit is a member of the Holy Trinity in heaven and the foundation of the holy trinity of God's gumbo here on earth: salt, light, and Spirit.

So I want to know . . . are you hungry?

HEART CHECK

- Does your heart posture tend to line up more with the story in Genesis 11 or Acts 2? When you are honest with yourself, are you striving to make a great name for yourself or are you striving for unity? Where do you see this in your life?
- What moments did you notice this week where people appeared to be outcasts or uncomfortable? How can you invite them in and help them feel comfortable in those moments?

- What is one way you can be the salt that brings out everyone else's flavors this week? How can your presence in someone's life honor the person God made them to be?

Father, I come asking You to increase my appetite to embrace those who are different from me. And give me eyes to see those who are far from me. As I acknowledge my own individuality, use me to play my part in Your kingdom by embracing diversity that ultimately brings this world to a place of unity. Reveal the areas in my life where being comfortable may have limited my ability to both represent and expand Your kingdom. I ask that with the help of the Holy Spirit, You help me to live beyond myself and love beyond my personal preferences. I desire to bring out the God colors and the God flavors of the world. Give me eyes to see people as You see them and love them as You love them. Use me as an essential ingredient in this big pot of God's gumbo.

SIX

GOD'S MASTERPIECE

Love looks for lines so that it can be defined.

"When did you two fall in love?"

Irene and I were sitting on a panel in front of hundreds of people at a marriage conference when we were asked that question. The conversation was just getting going, and the moderator thought he was throwing us an easy question to get us started.

But as soon as he asked that question, I lost it. I broke down and started crying.

"Six and a half years ago," I said through tears. "We fell in love six and a half years ago."

The moderator looked at me with a confused expression on his face. He didn't know what to say in response. The entire room went silent as everyone began doing the mental math. Because at the time, Irene and I had been married twenty-two years. How could we have just fallen in love six and a half years ago?

The moderator wasn't sure what to do, so I went on to explain that six and a half years ago Irene and I thought our marriage was over. At that point we had been struggling for years. We had learned to exist side by side, but we weren't happy. Eventually the silent resentment turned into vicious words of hate. We were getting into arguments every night, and that anger and those fights led us both to unhealthy vices to try to cope with what was going on. As I turned to food and Irene turned to alcohol, our relationship began to head to a dark place.

Irene's drinking started becoming a problem and my anger and my weight were spiraling out of control. I could preach to thousands, but I couldn't talk to the one I lay next to every night.

I didn't feel loved.

She didn't feel loved.

We were divided. And in our minds the only solution to the division was divorce.

A common reason given at the top of divorce papers is "irreconcilable differences." That's what Irene and I had. Differences we could not reconcile. Lines were drawn between us; our differences had turned to indifference for each other, which drove us apart.

And it was in that dark and lonely place six and a half years prior to that marriage conference that I learned what it truly means to love.

WHAT IS LOVE?

The word *love* gets thrown around a lot these days. People use that word to describe how they feel about everything from food to furniture.

But the Bible paints a much bigger and more beautiful picture of what love really is.

Scripture is full of example after example of people sinning and turning away from God. Throughout the course of this book, I've intentionally given you several examples of this, because our sin is the thing that creates separation. Ever since Adam and Eve ate from the tree in the garden, our shortcomings have created division between us. Our failures create rifts that separate us from God and from one another.

Sin creates lines.

But the really good news (and the point of this entire book) is that God's love does not stay within those lines. That's the message of the Bible from Genesis to Revelation. Our mistakes may have created separation, but God saw us at our ugliest and most broken moments and still loved us.

From our vantage point on earth, our sin created an irreconcilable difference between us and God. Fortunately, though, God went to great lengths to reconcile the irreconcilable. John 3:16 tells us, "For God so loved the world that he gave his one and only Son, that whoever believes in him shall not perish but have eternal life."

Why was God so passionate about fixing what we broke?

One word: *love.*

God saw us when we were at our lowest point, and He still chose to love us. Scripture says, "But God demonstrates his own love for us in this: While we were still sinners, Christ died for us" (Romans 5:8). While we were unlovable, God sent Jesus on a mission, to step over the line of heaven and come to earth, to bridge the gap between us and Him.

God didn't wait for us to clean up our act before He loved us. He didn't ask us to rearrange our lines before He loved us. Instead He saw us at our most broken state; He saw our ugliness, and He decided to love us in the midst of it. He decided to lay down His life, to die for us in order to shatter any division that came between us. He loved us so much that He went to great lengths to pay the price for our sins.

That's what love looks like.

God's love never stayed inside the lines of hate, preference, or background. It never stayed inside the lines of stereotypes or mis-judgments. Since the beginning, God's love has been instituted to bring man back into relationship with God.

When you watch the news today, it feels like our world is full of irreconcilable differences. It's easy to look at all the division and believe that we are all heading for a worldwide divorce. But I'm convinced that it doesn't have to be that way, because we serve a God who can reconcile the irreconcilable. There is a solution to this problem, and the solution is love.

But as great as that sounds on paper, let's be real: choosing love is not easy. And that's why all throughout this book, I keep reminding you that whenever loving gets challenging, we must come back to where love began. We have to come back to God.

LOVE STARTS WITH GOD

Six and a half years before that marriage conference, Irene and I saw each other's ugly sides. We came face-to-face with our lowest lows. We stood on either side of a massive chasm that felt like it was going to keep us apart forever.

In the midst of our marriage struggles, I sat on a couch and told my counselor every reason why I felt like I needed to call it quits. I explained every reason why I felt like the division between us was too great to lead to anything other than divorce.

My counselor listened patiently as I spoke my piece. Then she responded, "If you don't work this out, the new Irene won't get a chance to heal the [relationship] wounds that the old Irene created."

And then I got in my car to drive away and I got a call from a good friend. As I shared with him about my troubled marriage, this friend who loves both Irene and me said, "You will never get the wife you want until you love the wife you have."

When my friend used the word *love*, he wasn't using it lightly. He wasn't using it the way so many people do today; he was talking about the truest sense of the word *love*. The kind that would drive me to jump over any division that stood between my wife and me and fight to bring us back together. He wasn't talking about a feeling. He was talking about a decision.

I had to decide to love the one I laid next to every night, the one I had committed to, the one I had vowed to love no matter what. Through thick and thin, sick and sin, I committed to loving this person.

And through that brutal process, I finally realized that I would never be able to show my wife the love she deserved until I was able to receive the love God had for me. You can't give away something that you haven't first received. Choosing to love others is too difficult to do unless you first experience God's love yourself.

In Matthew 22 Jesus summarized the entire Bible in one breath. He said, "'Love the Lord your God with all your heart and with all your soul and with all your mind.' This is the first and greatest commandment. And the second is like it: 'Love your neighbor as yourself.' All the Law and the Prophets hang on these two commandments" (vv. 37–40).

That's it.

Our calling is to love one another.

But before we can do that, we must first love God, because it's impossible to share this love with one another if we don't first love God and receive God's love.

Love starts with God because as the Bible reminds us, "God is love" (1 John 4:16). Think about that for a second. God doesn't just try to love. He doesn't just love us when we love Him. He simply is love. Love is not a characteristic or an alias; love is who God is.

God is love, so He couldn't help it. Love has an innate desire to share itself. It cannot be love unless it is shared. It cannot be love unless it is received and felt by someone else. It cannot be love without redemption and restoration being its end goal. God is love!

God stepped over the line of what was incomprehensible. God stepped over the line of what was unexplainable. God stepped over the line that separated us from Him. And God instituted a plan to show us how to also step over the line. He sent His Son Jesus to step over the line of eternity and enter into humanity.

That kind of love is incomprehensible. Especially at the end of Jesus' ministry when He was hated, beaten, spit upon, and then hung on a cross, He didn't stop loving.

God's plan from the beginning was to show us that there is nothing we can do that will separate us from His love. In his letter to the Romans, Paul said it this way: "For I am convinced that neither death nor life, neither angels nor demons, neither the present nor the future, nor any powers, neither height nor depth, nor anything else in all creation, will be able to separate us from the love of God that is in Christ Jesus our Lord" (Romans 8:38–39).

That's the kind of love we are supposed to be carrying into the world. A love with no lines. When Jesus tells us to love our neighbor, He's not just telling us to tolerate them. He's calling us to go to great lengths and step over lines to love them.

To do that successfully you have to realize that God has created each one of us as a part of His masterpiece.

MASTERPIECE

When I was young, I loved coloring books. Remember, I had ADHD, so whenever we left the house, my mom would bring coloring books and crayons along with us and hand them to me whenever I needed something to focus on.

I'd sit there for hours, doing my best to turn that page into something beautiful. And then I'd hand it to my mom thinking I had just completed a masterpiece. But my mom always had the same feedback about my art: "You've got to stay in the lines."

I remember looking at my sister's picture one day and thinking how beautiful it was. She had stayed in the lines. Not only that, she had pressed the crayon into the boundaries and made them even stronger, then shaded within the lines.

To my mom, that was a masterpiece.

You see, since we were young, we've all been told to stay inside the lines that other people have created. We've been taught that success looks like obeying the boundaries that other people have created. And we've grown up hearing that coloring inside the lines is how masterpieces are formed.

But love doesn't stay in the lines. Love doesn't dig deeper and deeper into our opinions. Love does not press our ideologies harder and harder around our in-groups.

God's love doesn't work like a coloring book.

Did you know that God sees you as a masterpiece?

When you look around at all the different, diverse people in this world, you are looking at the tapestry of heaven. Picasso, Michelangelo, and van Gogh were all talented, but they were just shadows of the original artist. Yahweh looked down on a blank canvas, and He began to paint. He created a big and diverse world full of lots of different shapes, sizes, and colors. He created us all with our own idiosyncrasies, personalities, and opinions. And then He stepped back and called it really good.

We are the abstract art of God's creation!

I know it's not always in the lines, but that's the point of abstract art. That's the beauty of it—we are God's masterpieces.

It reminds me of the song "Jesus Loves the Little Children" that is sung in Sunday schools every week:

> *Jesus loves the little children,*
> *All the children of the world;*
> *Red and yellow, black and white,*
> *They are precious in His sight,*
> *Jesus loves the little children of the world.*[1]

If we could just understand that truth. If we could just learn to apply the lessons we learned in Sunday school to life as adults, I wonder what would change.

We are all fearfully and wonderfully made. When God chose our skin colors, He didn't make a mistake. We are the abstract art of God. And until we embrace how different we are, we will not understand just how valuable we are.

The artist was in love with all the colors.

And now the world gets a chance to sit back and enjoy this masterpiece.

EVEN THE UGLY PARTS

The relationship between Irene and me didn't start to change until we were able to look at each other (even the ugly parts) and learn to see each other for who we truly are: God's masterpieces.

In order to move forward together, we first had to accept and embrace each other right where we were. "For better or for worse" is not just fancy wordplay that sounds good in vows; it's a real-life picture of what it looks like to truly love another.

Irene's upbringing was completely different from mine. And Irene and I show and experience love in completely different ways. But we didn't realize that at the time.

Six and a half years before that marriage conference we both had a picture of what we thought love looked like. We had a nice, neat category for love in our minds, and we were both doing our best to color within those lines. We were expressing love the way we understood it as opposed to learning how each other received it.

The lesson we had to learn is that love was never meant to stay within our own lines. When I was young, my mom taught me that I was supposed to color in the lines. I was applying that same principle to my relationship with my wife. The problem was, my picture for what love was supposed to be was very different from her picture for what love was supposed to be.

To love each other we had to stop staying inside our own lines and our own definitions of love. We had to step outside the lines and learn how to truly love each other.

A simple example of this is seafood. When we met, Irene couldn't stand seafood. She didn't grow up eating it, and she couldn't understand why anyone would ever choose a seafood restaurant. We could've decided to continue coloring in the lines and avoid getting seafood on date nights, but instead, I reached across the line and introduced her to it. And she got out of her comfort zone and was open to trying it. Eventually she fell in love with it. Now it's one of our favorite things to do on date nights.

I had lines made up in my mind. I was done trying to love her, and I was determined that nothing was ever going to change. But love was the antidote. Love was prescribed. Love was needed. And love is what had to be applied.

Today Irene and I are doing better than ever before. Our marriage has never been healthier, and our love for each other has never been stronger. Irene hasn't touched a drink in six and a half years, and I am working through so much of my inner pain that was driving me away from her.

When we began to see each other the way God sees us, things started to change.

When we began to not just accept but embrace our differences, things began to change.

When we began to move our love outside the lines we once had, things began to change.

Getting to this point has taken a lot of work, but when you love someone, you put in the work and fight for them.

IS LOVE WORTH THE FIGHT?

As a teen I attended the high school that my father and his classmates had desegregated. The education system had drawn a hard line in the sand, and my father and his friends were forced to step over that line. This wasn't their decision; the decision was made for them. And, unproperly prepared, ended up hurting them.

One day they went to one high school, and the next day they got on a bus and went to a brand-new one. There was no preparation, no diversity training, nothing. One day my father was in a place of familiarity, the next day he and his friends were walking through halls being called ugly names they had never been called before. Overnight his whole world as a teenager shifted and he had to adapt. There was no one to walk him through it, as he and his friends were pioneering it.

As you can imagine, the experience was incredibly painful. He was stepping across a line that hadn't been stepped over before, and it brought on a lot of pain.

It was a huge step forward for his town, but it cost my father and many others so much.

We were talking about that experience awhile back, and he admitted that as a teen he would often wonder if they would've been better off staying segregated. That's how difficult it was for him. As he walked through the halls being called names, he'd find himself thinking the pain wasn't worth it.

Today we celebrate (and possibly romanticize) the process of integrating the school system. But for those who had to live through it, it was disorienting and disrupting.

That's the tension, isn't it?

If choosing love were easy, everyone would be doing it. And if carrying that love outside the lines were simple, I wouldn't need to write this book.

When my father was a teenager, he was facing the same predicament that so many of us find ourselves in today. Integration is possible, but it can also be incredibly difficult. Letting things remain segregated and separated is so much easier.

Like my father, we all have to ultimately make a decision. We must decide if love is worth the fight.

It would be so easy for me and for all of us to hate. It is so easy to stay separate. It would be easy to take our kickball and end the game because of the way the game is being played. It would be easy to despise. It would be easy to be discouraged. It would be easy to want to give up.

But what is hard is to love.

Think about the guy who has not had a voice and is so angry, and his heart is full of hate, so he turns a protest into a riot. Does he need love?

Or how about the police officer who has been taught how to hate. How to stereotype. How to profile. Does he need love?

And think about the skinhead. Does he need love?

What about when an olive-skinned man in a turban gets on a plane, and the couple in first class is bothered and jumps straight to judgment. Does that couple need love?

Yes, the answer is yes. And God's solution is that we would learn to step over our lines and be the change we want to see.

I know the system needs to change. I know the policies and procedures need to change. But I'm wondering, do we need to change? Do we need to receive something so that we can give it away?

Maybe the lines around our hearts need to be invaded with God's love so that the picket lines can be invaded with God's love.

Maybe we need to experience God's love internally so that people can experience God's love externally.

Love needs failure to prove that it can never fail.

Love needs hate to heal.

Love needs a fight to forgive.

Love needs injustice to bring in Jesus.

Love looks for lines so that it can be defined.

Love is a fight, but it's always worth it.

ONLY LOVE CAN DO THAT

Around the time Dr. Martin Luther King Jr. stood on the steps in Washington, DC, and delivered one of the greatest speeches in history in the middle of one of the most divided moments in our history, he gave a sermon called "Loving Your Enemies" at Dexter Avenue Baptist Church in Montgomery, Alabama. In the sermon he said these now famous words: "Darkness cannot drive out darkness; only light can do that. Hate cannot drive out hate; only love can do that."[2]

Love was King's message to a divided world. As his words echoed through churches, events, and the streets of the capital, our country was experiencing chaos and division. We didn't see one another as family. Generational strongholds had formed lines that looked insurmountable.

At the time reconciliation felt impossible. People were wondering how they could possibly learn to come together when they were experiencing so much hate. King's answer was just as true then as it is today. There is only one thing that breaks down division, and it's not hate.

In 2020, when Ahmaud Arbery was killed by two neighborhood vigilantes in broad daylight, I remember feeling so many different emotions.

I remember crying out of anger, frustration, and fear. But I'll never forget a conversation I had with my son. He came home one day after hanging out with his friends and needed to talk.

My son's friends, like so many others, were so angry and upset about what happened, they had decided they were drawing a line and they wanted him to choose a side. They wanted him to say that all White people are racist. He had a pencil with an eraser in his hand, but they wanted him to draw with a permanent marker. My son was confused and didn't know what to do because, remember, Irene is biracial—her mother is Zambian and her father is French Canadian.

I'll never forget my son's words. "Am I supposed to hate my grandfather now?"

That was the choice he felt he was being forced to make. He was just as frustrated as anyone else, but then he felt like he was being told to hate his own family.

At the end of our conversation, my son reached a conclusion that I'm so proud of him for. "It may be really hard to love," he said. "I may not be able to choose love for a while, but that doesn't mean I have to choose hate."

That's it right there.

Love is a lifelong journey, and the first step is deciding not to hate. I know it's hard to love at times, but refusing to hate is a great place to start.

My son didn't feel ready to love yet, but he was mature enough to realize his first step was choosing not to hate. Because you can't drive out hate with more hate—only love can do that.

THE ANTIDOTE

In the first chapter of this book, I told you about a rift in my family and in my own soul that I was experiencing in the Great Rift Valley. I realized in that valley that while I was so thankful for the foundation my parents had laid, it was time for me to keep moving forward.

When I returned from that trip, I was trying to heal, process, and reconcile everything I was feeling. For me art has always been one of the ways I like to do that. So I started an urban rock group called Locust Road. That's the street my parents' church was on, so I started that group to redeem the road and redeem the rift that was in my family.

One day I sat down to write and came up with what would become one of my favorite songs from that project. The song is called "The Antidote."

Because as I look around and see the division and the separation, it almost feels like there is no antidote to the problems we're facing. There are so many people on the other side of the line of how we vote, how we think, and how we see the world. Sometimes the void between us can feel so big that staying separate feels like the only solution. But there is a way forward. There is an answer for these differences. There is an antidote for this disease—the antidote is love.

The antidote to my father's struggles in his high school and the segregation that plagued so many during that era was love. The antidote to my son's social dilemma was love. And the antidote to Irene's and my struggling marriage was love.

There is a widespread infection in this world, but we've got the antidote.

The lyrics to the song are so near and dear to my heart, so as we get ready to head into these final chapters and learn how to love together, I want to share a few of the lyrics:

There's been an outbreak
The earth groans and quakes
Of mistakes made by a man who didn't know the high stakes
Confusion
What's the solution?
A critical condition, a symptom of spiritual pollution
Mediocrity, widespread hypocrisy
Humanity, idolatry, we need a remedy
Outrageous, deadly contagious, we can't contain this
A battle rages in the high places
Genocide children they cry
Black and whites divide
Preachers committing spiritual homicide
Churches weed out
They keep the sheep out

It's time to speak out, reach out
Blow the walls out before the time's out
I got the antidote
I got the antidote to set you free
Pain and agony are killing you slowly
I've got the cure for your disease so why you running from me?

—————— HEART CHECK ——————

- Can you relate to my marriage struggles at all? Even if you aren't married, have you ever had a great friendship or a relationship that survived a struggle?
- When are the moments you've found it most difficult to believe that you are God's masterpiece?
- If love is the antidote, what do you think it looks like for you personally to carry love into the world?

Father, thank You for all the relationships in my life.
Even the ones that are difficult sometimes. I know love is
the antidote, and I know that love comes from You. The

only reason I can love is because You first loved me. So would You remind me about Your love today, and would that reminder give me the strength and energy I need to be the antidote and carry Your love outside the lines?

SEVEN

BREAK THE STEREOTYPES

*Proximity is the goal, so stop letting stereotypes
keep you from getting close to people.*

Several years ago my family and I decided it was time for a vacation. We were all exhausted from our busy lives, and our schedules were so crazy that we weren't getting a lot of time to spend together.

We needed to get away.

The problem was we didn't have a whole lot of money. Our bank account was low, and we needed to figure out how to have some fun on a budget. So we loaded up our white GMC Acadia and headed to Virginia Beach. After a quick stop at Target to grab as many supplies as we could fit in our car, we crammed into a single hotel room and made the best of what we had.

The trip was amazing. We found a secluded beach we could hang out at during the day, and then we went and tried a bunch of new restaurants at night.

But on the final day of the trip, we decided to go big and take our kids to Hersheypark. Hersheypark is a famous amusement park that has something for everyone. The kids were excited about all the rides. I was just thinking about getting one of those giant turkey legs.

We got to the amusement park early and nearly wiped out our savings account paying the admission fees for the whole family and making sure our kids had the full experience. But when we got to the first big ride, we had to stand in line for what felt like forever. The park was already crowded, and the sun was scorching hot. And when we finally got to the front of the line, they informed us that Maya, my youngest daughter who was nine at the time, was not allowed to ride because she was too short.

"It's not fair," she protested, standing on her tippy toes to try to meet the height requirement. But it was no use. We had paid the full entrance fee for Maya, just like for everyone else, but because we were tall and she was short, she was excluded.

And it wasn't just that ride. The same thing happened all day long.

The park was packed full of rides for tall people, but people who were Maya's height only had a handful of options.

"It's not fair," she kept saying over and over again, trying to make sense of what was happening. "I don't understand."

My daughter was upset and confused—partially because she

wasn't allowed to go on all the fun rides, but mostly because she was treated differently than everyone else in our family. While we were allowed to ride, she was told she had to sit out.

Maya felt different.

And if you've ever experienced that feeling, you know how much it hurts.

A line was drawn in the amusement park. Hersheypark decided on a height, drew a line, and decided that everyone who was shorter than that mark was not allowed to ride. Four of us got to enjoy everything the park had to offer, while Maya was told she was only allowed to go to certain places and ride certain rides.

My family all went to the same amusement park. We all paid the same entrance fee and walked the same streets. We drove there together and stood in line together, but Maya's memories are different from ours. She was super upset watching her brother and sister have the time of their lives. It was too much for her little brain to process.

ADVANTAGES AND DISADVANTAGES

Did you know that it's possible to be in the same family and share the same events but have two completely different experiences?

What some people experience as an amazing day at an amusement park, other people experience as a lot of standing in long lines only to be told they don't meet the qualifications to enjoy what everyone else can enjoy.

At Hersheypark tall people have an advantage that short

people do not. There are rides that are only set up for tall people to ride.

Now, safety in an amusement park is one thing. I'm not trying to say we shouldn't have protocols set in place for rides to keep everyone safe. But I do think this is a good metaphor for what we are doing in the world today. I think my daughter's experience is a picture of the division we have in our society.

The system is set up in favor of tall people, but it can be really difficult for a tall person to see that or acknowledge it because it isn't affecting them negatively.

In case you haven't picked up on the metaphor yet, I'm not talking about height. I'm talking about race. In our nation there are inherent advantages to being White, and there are disadvantages to being a person of color.

Historically there have been several rides that people who look like me weren't allowed to go on because of the color of our skin. There are places we've been told we weren't allowed to visit because of the color of our skin. And there were certain stereotypes we had to learn to live with and work hard to overcome because of the color of our skin.

I've noticed that people who aren't immediately affected by those systems, lines, or stereotypes typically are not quick to acknowledge that they are real. The Bible tells us, "Everyone should be quick to listen, slow to speak and slow to become angry" (James 1:19). But oftentimes when I try to talk to a "tall person" about the system, someone who's not negatively impacted by it, they are slow to listen, quick to become angry, and even quicker to throw out balancing statements to try to explain why I am wrong.

When we were at Hersheypark, I watched my other kids do that exact thing throughout the course of the day. Maya was upset the entire time, and my other kids didn't understand why she was so aggravated. So on the car ride home, Irene and I got to lead a family discussion.

We let Maya explain to her siblings why something that seemed like a small thing in their minds was a big thing in hers. They didn't understand at first, but we got to explain to them that while they had the opportunity to ride any ride they wanted all day, their sister was forced to sit out.

It wasn't a fun-filled vacation for Maya; it was a reminder that there are certain lines drawn in this world that she wasn't allowed to cross. And lines that exclude you from the very thing that everyone else gets to experience are always painful.

We all had the same vacation, but her experiences were different. What some people believe is fair, other people experience as unfair. What some people call a fun day, other people call a frustrating day.

And until we are honest and humble enough to admit that two different people can experience one thing but have two different experiences with two different perspectives, stereotypes will continue to keep us from loving outside the lines.

THE DANGER OF STEREOTYPES

The year 2020 was difficult for our entire world.

The global pandemic hit hard and put everyone on edge.

But the great equalizing factor about the pandemic was that it affected everyone. We may have been scared, but at least we were all scared together. We all had experiences of fear, anxiety, and death. We were all in line together for food, toilet paper, and a vaccine. As scary as it was, it was somewhat comforting to be in it together. But then tragedy struck, and the lines of racism, political difference, and experience reminded us how divided our country has always been.

Ahmaud Arbery was killed while he was jogging through a predominantly White neighborhood; Breonna Taylor lost her life when police officers burst into her home; and George Floyd was killed by a White police officer on the street in broad daylight.

And suddenly I felt short again.

Imagine a short guy running in a neighborhood of tall people. And they are so unfamiliar with a short person that they assume he is a threat, so they shoot and kill him.

Imagine a tall police officer who grew to fear short people, so when he is called to investigate a short person, he jumps to a conclusion and holds him down in the street until he doesn't have any air left in his lungs.

That would be ridiculous, right?

This is the danger of stereotypes. They hurt more than just feelings; they get people killed.

Stereotypes are the views of the narrow-minded. They are the things we've made up, or the things we've been told about a person or place without having any actual proximity or personal experience. The thought that young Black men are up to no good or that Latinos are trying to take all our jobs are examples of stereotypes. They are harmful because instead of erasing lines, they look for ways to draw them deeper. Instead of looking to bring out the best in people, stereotypes search for the worst, and when they find any slipup or shortcoming that confirms their bias, they double down on it.

Stereotypes keep our nation divided, so it's time to have another family discussion. When we left Hersheypark, Irene and I needed to talk to our children. It's time for you and me to do the same thing.

This time the topic is the danger of stereotypes.

ANOTHER FAMILY DISCUSSION

Remember we've already established that we're all family in God's kingdom. So now it's time for you to take a seat at my dining room table and get really honest.

I'd like to share with you a few personal experiences with stereotypes that have marked me. I could tell you stories all day, but instead, I've picked three quick stories of my own experiences of feeling "too short." Of feeling perceived by others as not enough. Of feeling like I wasn't allowed to ride the same ride that everyone else was on.

But before we begin, remember the rules of family discussions: suspend your judgment and at least hear me out for these three stories. My goal is to show you what stereotypes can do to people on the receiving end. I want to challenge you to lean in to these stories and do your best to experience them from my perspective.

Story 1: What Inner City Are You From?

When I graduated from high school and was ready for my next step, I chose to attend a nearby Bible college in Phoenixville, Pennsylvania. My family and I packed everything I owned into my grandad's RV and drove from Maryland to Pennsylvania.

At the time the school had about a thousand students, but only about fifteen of us were Black. The first day on campus, there was a reception for all the new students and their families. While we were hanging out, getting a feel for my new school, the school president walked over to my family and me and asked, "What inner city are you guys from?"

The purpose of this school was to train future church leaders, but my first experience with the president of the school was him assuming that since I was Black, I must've been from the inner city. That's an example of a stereotype. Along the way this guy had decided that someone who looked like me was probably from the inner city, and he had believed that for so long that it had become second nature to him.

But we had lived in the suburbs our entire lives. Can you see why someone jumping to that conclusion based on a stereotype and the color of our skin can be hurtful? Especially when it is the president of the place that is supposed to be training up future church leaders.

The church is supposed to be the hope of the world. But is it the hope for the whole world or just the "tall" people?

Story 2: Chapel

I made a lot of friends in college, mostly White, and many of them became like brothers. We were tight. We did everything together on that campus.

One day we were in chapel as usual. Chapel was one of the staples in Bible college. We logged a lot of hours worshiping and listening to sermons in that sanctuary. But on this particular day, we couldn't focus.

We were trying and failing to pay attention to the message because we were all looking at something else. One of our teachers, a missions professor, was preaching, and everyone's attention was on his tie. It was a bad tie—one of those you get for Christmas or Father's Day.

No one dared say anything, but the giggles and whispers made it clear. We were all drawn to his tie. Then he began his talk.

Regardless of the tie, everything was going as expected. It was a standard chapel sermon, but as he finished up his second point and we were all ready for him to round the corner with his third point and close the service, he decided to try out a joke.

Unfortunately it was a racially insensitive joke that I'll never forget. He even used the N-word in the middle of it. You could feel the tension in the room, although he clearly couldn't because he went on.

I was the only Black guy in my row, and I felt like all the attention shifted from the bad tie to me. I felt like the bad tie.

People giggled, they were laughing, and at that moment, I realized the tension I felt was because there were fifteen people in that room who were likely hurting deeply, and everyone else didn't seem to be bothered.

All the friends I had made, the brotherhood I experienced daily, fell away like a curtain being pulled back on a window. I felt like I was on display. I suddenly felt like a stranger among my friends. I felt alone, like I did on the first day of school. I stood out like a sore thumb, and I could feel my friends looking to see my reaction. For one brief minute, I wished the ground would swallow me. There was nothing I could do. All this was going on in the seats as the professor continued and concluded chapel as if nothing had happened.

To this day I don't know if anything was ever said to him about it. And remember, he was the missions professor. It was his job to prepare people for missions, to literally go all over the world and enter different cultures to preach Christ, yet he had told a racist joke in a sermon. We are the ones called to bring people to life, not to shame.

He can take off his bad tie, and people will stop laughing at him. But what can I take off to get people to stop laughing at me or hating me based on the color of my skin? I can't take off my Black skin, nor do I want to.

But as I sat in that chapel, I felt like I was being reminded that I was too short to ride.

Story 3: The Basketball Court

Unfortunately that chapel was not the most uncomfortable confrontation I experienced in Bible college.

Not long after, I was playing pickup basketball with my

friends in the gymnasium. On that particular night my game was on fire. I was crushing everyone. The other team put a guy on me to defend me who barely knew how to play basketball.

If you've ever played against a guy who barely knows how to play, you know they typically play rough. He was fouling me left and right, and I was starting to get heated. So I called for the ball, crossed him over, and scored on him.

As soon as I did, his frustration reached a boiling point, and he turned around and called me the N-word to my face. That was the end of Bible college for me because I punched him so hard in the face that he ended up in the hospital, and I got kicked out for fighting.

The message that the kid was sending me was clear: even if I could beat him at basketball, he still believed he was better than me because of the color of my skin. He believed I was too short to ride the rides, and in a moment of frustration, he wanted to make sure he let me know it.

BACK TO THE TABLE

Now imagine you've been sitting at my dining room table with me having this family discussion. You just heard about three separate experiences where stereotypes both hurt and humiliated me.

And the most confusing part for me (you probably already picked this up) is that all three of those moments happened at Bible college.

That was the hardest part.

This was the place for people who felt called to prepare for ministry. This was a place where world-changers were being trained, yet they were being trained by those with such a limited worldview.

They were supposed to be in the business of disciple-making, but it was in that space that I experienced the most personally racist acts of my entire life. I would move on and stay in ministry, maintaining friends and relationships with different people from school, both White and Black, but the pain remained.

I still had an internal default thought toward any White pastor, especially if they were from the denomination of the school, believing that they all felt the same as that professor who taught in chapel that day and was never corrected.

And so, as you have sat around the family table listening to my stories, how are you feeling? Angry? Confused? Indifferent?

Have any of these stories pushed you or challenged you in any way?

Have any of them made you think differently about any experiences you've had?

Have any of them illuminated stereotypes you may hold on to that you didn't even realize you had?

Do you ever (intentionally or unintentionally) make people feel short? As if they aren't enough?

When you go out to eat with your coworkers and there is only one short person around, do you push them aside or do you go the extra mile to help them feel welcome?

If you only have a few short people in your neighborhood,

do you make sure they know they are just as important to your neighborhood as anyone else?

Or when you are driving through a neighborhood where mostly short people live, do you ever find yourself judging them? Or trying to make yourself feel tall by making them feel short?

The thing about harmful stereotypes is that the damage they do often goes unnoticed. Returning to that day at Hersheypark, most people, including Maya's siblings, didn't know how Maya was feeling. Similarly, most of the students at Bible college didn't know any of this happened to me or how it made me feel. Even some of my friends who went to school with me will read this and think, *What are you talking about? Bible college was amazing!*

Of course it was—for you. You were tall enough to go on all the rides. You didn't experience any of the lines because you were always on the right side of them.

My family talked a long time on our drive home from Hersheypark. The more we talked, the more our kids began to understand that their experience wasn't the only experience; it was just one perspective.

Part of being a human is learning how to see the world from other people's perspectives, from additional vantage points. If you are short, you have a completely different experience at the amusement park. You can't see as much. When people are tall, they think they have a better perspective. But it's not a better perspective—it's just a different perspective. It's one of many.

You and I can't change what happened, but what happened can change us. We can acknowledge that just because something is not our experience doesn't mean it wasn't experienced by someone else—and possibly experienced as being harmful or painful.

THE HOPE OF THE WORLD?

There are lots of stories I could've told you about the harm people's negative judgments have had on me, but I told you stories from Bible college on purpose.

The church is supposed to be the hope of the world, but the question is, whose world? Is the church only the hope of the world for tall people? Or is it the hope of the world for all people?

The apostle Paul made it clear that we should stop letting stereotypes draw lines in our family. In Galatians he wrote, "There is neither Jew nor Gentile, neither slave nor free, nor is there male and female, for you are all one in Christ Jesus" (3:28). It doesn't get much clearer than that. According to Paul, the family of God should all see one another as one.

We are all called to be unified.

But that doesn't mean we are supposed to be the same. Unity is not the same as uniformity. Our differences are one of the things that make us so unique and special. That's why Paul also likened the church to the body. "For just as the body is one and has many members, and all the members of the body, though many, are one body, so it is with Christ" (1 Corinthians 12:12 ESV).

We aren't called to uniformity, but we are called to unity.

Which means we aren't all going to be the same height. But we aren't supposed to draw hard lines of division and split ourselves up into separate groups. We aren't supposed to form stereotypes around different heights or let those differences divide us. Have we gotten to a place where we've decided it's just easier to let tall people do church in one place and short people do church in another place? Imagine what we could do together.

The church is supposed to be a place of unity and a picture of a world where we love across the lines. Where people are accepted for who they are. But at this particular Bible college, I experienced lines.

A lot of them.

The church is where there's supposed to be a space for everyone, tall and small. But instead I was excluded from some of the rides. I was told I didn't fit in. Through offhand comments, jokes, and words, I was told I didn't belong.

If the church is the hope of the world for all people, then no one should feel like a bad tie. No one should feel judged. No one should get called any word that would provoke them to anger based on their height. And certainly, no one should be called a racial slur.

When the church remains divided, it won't move forward. Jesus said it like this: "If a kingdom is divided against itself, that kingdom cannot stand" (Mark 3:24 ESV).

Whether you attend church or are a church leader, it's important for you to hear me and think about this: the church is supposed to be the hope of the world, but oftentimes it is a place of division. How can you expect someone to call you pastor if you fail to even acknowledge the pain of your sheep?

Are you willing to sit and listen? Are you open to learning

from and hearing someone else's perspective? And are you willing to do that with an open mind, being ready to admit when you are wrong?

There was this little rhyme I remember learning in Sunday school, the one where we folded our hands together and said, "Here is the church, here is the steeple, open the doors, and see all the people." But when I open the doors to my "church," all my "people" look like me, and I bet yours do too. My people are brown, a little ashy, and even a little chubby. What do your people look like? What about the church you currently attend or periodically attend? Look around—what do they look like? How do they live? How do they vote? All the same?

The church in our hands right now looks too much like us. Martin Luther King Jr. once famously said, "I think it is one of the tragedies of our nation, one of the shameful tragedies, that eleven o'clock on Sunday morning is one of the most segregated hours, if not the most segregated hours, in Christian America."[1]

The church in Jesus' hands looked very different. You can tell just by looking at the disciples He chose, the places He visited, and the people He dined with. Jesus did not represent a ministry with rituals and political affiliations. He wasn't even bound to a building. His church on earth was made up of people from all different places and all walks of life, united in one thing—that He was the Messiah, Son of the living God.

If the church is going to indeed be the hope of the world that we are called to be, we are going to need to learn how to step over lines and have proximity with those who don't look or think like us.

PROXIMITY IS THE POINT

One day Jesus was walking with His disciples when He asked them two questions. The first one was, "Who do people say the Son of Man is?" (Matthew 16:13).

Jesus wanted to know what people were saying about Him. I picture the disciples all looking at one another nervously before one spoke up: "Some say John the Baptist; others say Elijah; and still others, Jeremiah or one of the prophets" (v. 14).

But then Jesus changed the stakes with His second question: "'But what about you?' he asked. 'Who do you say I am?'" (v. 15).

What's the difference between those two questions? Proximity. The first question was about people around town, but the second question was directed to the twelve disciples who knew Jesus and went everywhere with Him.

This was Peter's time. In a rare moment of wisdom, Peter spoke up and answered correctly, "You are the Messiah, the Son of the living God" (v. 16).

Jesus was happy with the answer. Peter, the guy who usually said and did all the wrong things, answered perfectly. That's what proximity does. The responses of those who hadn't been near Jesus weren't based on experiences; they were just based on what they had heard. But Peter had had a revelation based on experience.

We can't define something we haven't had proximity with.

This is the basis of stereotypes. Stereotypes are conclusions we jump to without first having proximity.

That's why news channels are full of stereotypes. They give

people an opportunity to form opinions about certain groups of people from the comfort of their living rooms. [Insert your preferred news station] looks for examples that reaffirm whatever stereotypes they are selling so that the viewer can continue to draw a line around their living room and form their decisions based off of what's being reported instead of relationships with real human beings.

My third year of college, a freshman told me I was the very first Black person he had ever seen in real life. One day at the lunch table, he commented on how my palms were white. He had no idea. It was his first time being near a Black guy.

He'd had a lack of proximity his entire life.

We cannot reach people that we are far from. If we can't even see one another's differences, we'll fail to understand our different experiences.

In order to live outside the lines, you have to go outside the lines. Proximity is the goal, so stop letting stereotypes keep you from getting close to people.

THE PROCESS THAT LEADS TO PREJUDICE

When I'm speaking to a large group, there's an exercise I like to do to help them understand the danger of stereotypes. I ask everyone who is listening to raise their hand if they like being comfortable. And typically everyone raises their hand. Next I ask them to raise their hand if they prefer to be comfortable. Again everyone in the room will raise their hand.

Everyone likes and prefers to be comfortable. The problem arises when you allow your preference to be comfortable to turn into your standard. Because it's one thing to enjoy being around people you are comfortable with; it's another thing to expect it.

That's why we form in-groups.

We surround ourselves with people who look, think, and act like us so we can speak openly and freely because it's comfortable. But then the people we are comfortable with become the people we prefer to be around. And eventually, given enough time, our preference becomes our standard.

Comfort begins as something we like, then it becomes what we prefer, and finally, it becomes our standard.

Once surrounding ourselves with people who think and look like us becomes our standard, we start to lose proximity with everyone else. If our in-group consists only of tall people, then we don't have any proximity with short people, and if our in-group is full of short people, we stop having proximity with tall people.

This is the process that leads to prejudice.

By the end of our day at Hersheypark, Maya was so fed up with the system that she kept saying she just wanted to go to an all-kids amusement park, where tall people weren't allowed to get on the rides.

That's real.

I've felt that way. I've had moments when I've realized that since there aren't as many rides for me, it would be so much easier to just go to a park that is only for people who look like me.

That's what the Enemy wants us to do. He doesn't want us to

get to know those family members we haven't even met yet. He doesn't want true unity.

If you've found yourself being told you aren't allowed to ride, have you grown bitter and decided to only surround yourself with other people who are in your predicament? And have you decided that all tall people are the same and that none of them recognize short people? Or even that all tall people hate short people?

That way of thinking will keep us from having proximity.

People don't usually start out with prejudice in their hearts; it's something we learn along the way. Because if we never have proximity with people who aren't like us, it becomes very easy for prejudice to take root. And now, since we have no proximity to anyone who is not tall, we stereotype everyone we are not comfortable with. Once we stereotype those people, we prejudge them because we don't have proximity.

Compare that to Jesus, who looked at crowds and had compassion for them. He didn't separate Himself from the group and make assumptions about them; instead, He had compassion for them and moved toward them.

If you are feeling uneasy, I don't want you to think I'm calling you racist. Your conviction could just mean that you are comfortable. But is that true about you? Are you comfortable? And has your comfort turned into preferences? And have your preferences turned into standards? And have your standards caused you to stereotype people? And in your stereotypes, are you prejudging? And has your prejudging turned into racism?

If Jesus had been okay with comfort, He would've stayed in heaven. But He smashed the stereotypical mindset of comfort by coming to earth and hanging out with people He should not have been comfortable with. He even hung out with someone who would betray Him.

He never operated in stereotypes.

Even with Bartimaeus, a blind guy who was begging for help. It was obvious to everyone what he was asking for help with, but Jesus took the time to ask him, "What do you want me to do for you?" (Mark 10:51).

Really, Jesus? What are you talking about? He's blind. Help him see.

But could it be that Jesus didn't want to put him in the category of being tall or short; He just wanted Bartimaeus to know that He saw him first and foremost as a human being who deserved love and respect?

Jesus didn't let stereotypes move Him away from people.

Instead, He let love move Him toward people.

Love compelled Jesus across all lines and boundaries. It moved Him to sit with people who didn't look like Him, talk with people who didn't think like Him, and eat with people who didn't believe the same things He believed.

Love led Jesus to smash all the harmful stereotypes of the day in order to see people for who they really were. And although it took His disciples some time, they eventually allowed love to break down their stereotypes too.

Stereotypes do more harm than we realize. They solidify

lines and cement boundaries by looking for reasons to ignore the positives and reaffirm the negatives.

If you want to love outside the lines, you can't be apathetic toward stereotypes.

Like Jesus, you must be willing to call out stereotypes and break them. Shine a light on them, expose them, and then start loving the people on the other side of the lines.

HEART CHECK

- Can you resonate with Maya's experience at Hersheypark? When have you been told you couldn't do something or go somewhere that other people were allowed to go?
- Have you ever felt like the bad tie that everyone is staring at? What do you remember about that experience? How did it make you feel?
- What did you learn about stereotypes while reading this chapter? If you are being honest, what are some of the negative stereotypes you've believed, at one time or another, about a certain group of people? Where did that stereotype come from and how can you move past it?

Dear Lord, You created us to be one family. However, the negative stereotypes we have about one another keep us from doing that fully. But I don't want to have any of these negative stereotypes in my life, so would You teach me how to see them, identify them, confess them, and get rid of them? Search me, God, and know my heart; test me and see if there is any offensive way in me, and lead me in the way everlasting.

EIGHT

BE IN ON IT

*It's time for the body of Christ to be a part
of the solution instead of the pollution.*

When our kids were a bit younger, Irene and I were on vaca-
tion by ourselves when we got a series of texts from them. We
were trying to relax, but we could immediately tell that something was seriously wrong.

They were sending us screenshots of posts from classmates
who were using racial slurs on social media and saying that Black
people shouldn't be at their school.

Naturally our kids were upset. These were people they sat
in class with, shared lunchrooms with, and even worshiped in
chapel services with at this Christian school. I also got upset. I

know these attitudes exist in the world, but I had hoped for my kids to be kept from it a bit longer. I asked them if they knew who the people were.

When they told me, I was taken aback. The prime offender wasn't just someone they knew; it was someone I knew well. He was the son of a pastor in the same city I pastored in. The pastor was a friend of mine. I had to sit with myself for a minute and pastor myself. This hurt.

If this is how the kid feels, is this how his dad feels? I didn't want to allow my mind to speculate or even go there. But after I took a moment, I decided to call him and have a conversation with him because I did not want this to divide us.

He and his wife were genuinely apologetic. They weren't making excuses and they didn't try to cover it up. In fact, the incident was so important to them that they came over to our house with their son as soon as we got home from vacation. Irene and I talked with them and cried together for hours, and then, around midnight, Jaden came downstairs and talked to their son right in the middle of the living room.

Jaden told him, "I don't know why you said what you said. That is messed up. But I forgive you and if you come back to school, I am going to make sure that no one hurts you."

If anyone ever needs a lesson on how to love outside the lines, they need to meet Jaden Rollins.

Jaden could've easily grown bitter and let those hurtful and hateful words ruin their friendship. But instead he refused to let the offense have the last say. He reached a hand across the dividing line. And as soon as he did, the walls came down. Their family began asking us how this experience made us feel, and we ended up talking late into the night.

Even though Jaden was the one who got hurt, he reached over that invisible fence and initiated a conversation that began the process of reconciliation.

That's what this chapter is all about. For the previous few chapters, we've been exploring the invitation to carry our love outside the lines. But now it's time to get even more practical and learn how to have conversations with people who don't look or think like we do.

Few things erase the lines that we put up between one another faster than conversations. Because when we have conversations with people who don't look like us, we get the chance to see the world from their perspective. We get to learn about the backstory that drives their behaviors.

BE IN ON IT

The apostle Paul was great at having conversations with diverse groups of people. He was a missionary who took the Word into lots of different countries and cultures. He was an expert at learning to see the world from other points of view. So how did he bring the gospel outside the lines? In 1 Corinthians, he shared the key to his effectiveness in sharing the gospel with other cultures. I love Paul's CliffsNotes from The Message translation:

Even though I am free of the demands and expectations of everyone, I have voluntarily become a servant to any and all in order to reach a wide range of people: religious, nonreligious, meticulous moralists, loose-living immoralists, the defeated, the demoralized—whoever. I didn't take on their way of life. I kept my bearings in Christ—but I entered their world and tried to experience things from their point of view. I've become just about every sort of servant there is in my attempts to lead those I meet into a God-saved life. I did all this because of the Message. I didn't just want to talk about it; I wanted to be *in* on it! (9:19–23)

I love that last line: "I wanted to be in on it."

Paul couldn't just stay at home where he was comfortable; he wanted "to reach a wide range of people." Because he wanted to be in on it!

Paul couldn't just have conversations with people who agreed with him; instead, he talked to "religious, nonreligious, meticulous moralists, loose-living immoralists, the defeated, the demoralized—whoever." Because he wanted to be in on it!

Paul couldn't stay within the lines of what he knew; instead, he "entered their world and tried to experience things from their point of view." Because he wanted to be in on it!

And Paul couldn't just keep to himself; instead, he "[became] just about every sort of servant there is in my attempts to lead those I meet into a God-saved life." Because he wanted to be in on it!

What about you? Are you ready to be in on it? If so, you

are going to have to learn how to step out of your comfort zone and have conversations with people who don't look like you, talk like you, or vote like you. You are going to need to learn to put down your differences and find common ground with people.

That's what this chapter is about. Paul's way was diversity with the goal of unity. His way was about entering any and everyone's world to experience it from their point of view. This is the way of the kingdom; this is how we can be in on it.

And like Paul, it starts with learning to have life-giving conversations, so here are a few simple places to start.

1. Enter Their World

Paul was willing to cross over any line necessary to enter other people's worlds. We have to realize there are opportunities to enter into people's worlds all around us; we just have to keep our eyes open.

Awhile back Irene and I were driving down the highway and I saw a man who was driving recklessly. He was speeding and bobbing in and out of lanes, and as my wife and I watched, I mused, "He's either going to hurt someone or hurt himself driving like that."

I couldn't let him out of my sight, though. His recklessness got my attention. I called the police to let them know what was happening and where, and I stayed on him. Because I was truly afraid for his life, my agenda became secondary at that moment.

Sure enough, one of his attempts to weave into a lane resulted in him flipping over not once but sixteen times down the highway. I wasn't thinking (and I *do not* recommend doing this)—I pulled over and I ran to him. He was trapped, and I don't know how but I got that door open and pulled him out.

He was White; I am Black.

He appeared to be older; I was younger.

He looked and acted like he was high; I was sober.

But none of that mattered in the moment. In all that made us different, I looked at the blood pouring out of his face and the blood coming out of my hand (I seemed to have cut myself at some point getting him out)—our blood, the life force running through our bodies, was the same. He was a human, alive, and had a need.

And my love compelled me to break into his world—and his car—and interact with him.

I could've ignored his reckless driving, justified in my mind that it was his fault, and continued on with my day. But as followers of Jesus, we must stop letting fear keep us inside the lines. We must stop being afraid to break through barriers and form relationships with people who don't look like us.

This car accident was an extreme circumstance, but when we decide to keep our eyes open every day, we'll begin to notice there are opportunities all around us to step over lines and enter into other people's worlds. Whether it is the person sitting next to you on the plane, the cashier at the grocery store, or the coworker in the cubicle next to you, there are always opportunities to enter people's worlds and initiate conversations.

We just have to keep our eyes open!

2. Empathize with Everyone

The second thing Paul was great at was empathizing with all the people he interacted with.

Empathy allows us to move past any unforgiveness or bitterness we may have against a person or a people group and engage in real conversations with them.

During his ministry, Paul had a rough ride. Between the beatings, the imprisonments, the stonings, and the death threats, Paul had plenty of reasons to stay bitter at different groups of people. But he didn't seem to carry that bitterness with him. Instead he released it. He moved on and seemed to have empathy for everyone everywhere he went.

When we harbor bitterness in our hearts, we will ignore opportunities to have conversations. Or at least we will ignore life-giving conversations. When we are bitter, we may say a few words to a person, but we won't enter into the life-changing conversations this chapter is all about.

If we want to have conversations that lead us to love outside the lines, we first have to learn how to forgive.

In the last chapter we had a family discussion about some of the difficult experiences I had at Bible college. The truth is, I held on to that pain and anger for almost two decades. But several years ago, God led me on a journey to address my unforgiveness.

I went out to Wyoming on a wilderness trip with a group of about forty pastors I knew. While there I struck up a conversation with one of the guides who was teaching me how to fly-fish. Fly-fishing is hard, but the questions he asked me while we were fishing were even harder.

He was a white guy, and I could tell he hadn't had a whole lot of proximity with diversity. But he jumped right in and started asking me questions, expressing how he wanted to help but just didn't really know how. He asked me some vulnerable questions, and I believe that we should have these safe spaces to work our issues out together. He shared that he'd felt intimidated around Black people, didn't understand why, and didn't want to feel that way. My heart went out to him because that kind of honesty and vulnerability is what God works with. He was teaching me how to fly-fish, but I was giving him a lesson in diversity on the fly.

Later in that trip an opportunity to hike a mountain came up. Have you ever had a moment when you didn't want to do a thing but you also wanted to do the thing at the same time? That's how I felt. It looked hard. This mountain was ridiculous and not my first idea of a good time. I did not want to do it, but something inside of me was pushing me to go for it. I felt like I would be missing an opportunity if I didn't. In that moment I imagined feeling accomplished for doing it, for getting some exercise, and having some bragging rights when I got home to my wife. This is what I thought the opportunity was.

A small group of us was brave enough to take on this feat. It was me, a few other friends, and an older gentleman who was a counselor. As we journeyed up, one of them turned around to return to camp, and the others went up ahead, until it was just me and the older gentleman.

He and I kept pace together, and we began to talk and share our experiences. He asked me to share my story, and we got on the topic of Bible college. I ended up telling him what happened in chapel that day and how I eventually got kicked out for fighting. I could feel his grief and remorse.

He started to silently tear up as he said to me, "I'm sorry that was your experience. I'm a part of that denomination and I am working hard to try to change those things. I don't know the person who said those things, but I just want to say, I'm sorry. That shouldn't be your experience."

This man had empathy for my experience.

He didn't know me outside of us hiking together, but he cried and apologized for something he never did. His apology gave me an opportunity to be aware of how deeply the situation had affected me.

I realize now the internal battle for me to climb this mountain had a much more divine intention behind it. This climb wasn't to gain a little bit of exercise and experience. This climb was to exercise my heart in a different way and remove my unforgiveness. His apology not only showed me my bitterness but also gave me the opportunity to release forgiveness and with God's grace remove the anger that had resided in my heart for over twenty years.

Once I did that, I realized the bitterness was replaced with empathy.

I'm grateful to him for his humility and availability, and I am grateful to God for the opportunity. The redemption continued when I went on to find the guy I had hit over twenty years ago on that basketball court. I called him and apologized to him. The conversation went great. He remembered me and actually followed me on social media. "Don't worry about it," he said. "I see all the good stuff you're doing. Keep it up."

I remembered as a young man feeling so justified in my physical actions. Between the bad-tie guy and the basketball guy, I was so hurt and I felt voiceless. At that time it made me feel like all White people, especially those from this denomination, had some racism in them.

But as a more seasoned disciple of Christ, one who has climbed some mountains literally and spiritually, I have learned the blessing of forgiveness that leads to unity. That anger is gone, and the strongholds have been pulled down, all through forgiveness.

And it's been replaced with empathy.

What about you? Do you have any unforgiveness in your heart that is keeping you from having conversations with people who are not in your in-group? Where were you hurt? Where were you intimidated? Where were you oppressed? Where is it?

Find it, and let's forgive it.

Let's release forgiveness over that to get you into a place of peace. A place where you can enjoy relationships without a wall separating you. A place of unity with others, a place where God commands a blessing. Because if you want to be in on it and have life-giving and line-erasing conversations, you have to have the type of empathy that can only come from being willing to forgive!

3. Experience What They Experience

When my wife was pregnant with our first child, we were so excited. We were all in. I dreamed about what kind of dad I would be. This really was the most exciting time in our lives up to that point. We did all the things new parents did: we went to the stores to create a baby registry with all the little items, we were all about getting her little room ready, and we went to Lamaze class.

In our first class they talked about all the things the mother would go through during birth, and I wondered why I was there. I mean, in past generations, the men stayed in a separate room and waited until it was over. It seemed like my only job was to rub her back, hold her a certain way, and remind her to breathe. Remind her to breathe? Who forgets breathing? Why would she need a reminder to breathe? On the day Irene went into labor, it became 100 percent clear to me how important my job was.

On a cold day in December my wife experienced intense pressure and unbearable pain, and she screamed like I had never heard before. As her husband I could have left the room and abandoned my position. But this is a new day, and husbands have the opportunity to support our wives. Our sole job may be miniscule but when it matters most it's necessary.

My only job was to help her breathe through a pain that I will never experience. My job was to do everything I could to enter into her world and be there to share the experience with her.

My job was to support her and help keep her grounded, and it bonded us in a new way.

They don't teach you in Lamaze how to minimize the pain for the person giving birth; they teach you to enter in and be completely aware of what is happening in the room and give support to the person giving birth. I didn't look at my wife and say,

"It really doesn't hurt that much" or, "In my grandmother's day they did not have the medicine you have and she was fine."

They do teach you to read the room, listen to the doctor, hold your wife, and remind her to breathe in a way that supports what she needs to do to get through the pain of childbirth. To breathe in a way that doesn't cause her to cut off air supply to her vital organs, to breathe in a way that keeps her aware and pushes out this new life that is meant to come into the world.

It is impossible to convince someone else how bad your pain is. When I go to the doctor I am asked, "Where is the pain?" and "On a scale of one to ten, how bad is the pain?" Just as I've never gone to a doctor and been told that my pain is not real or that it is really a three when I say it is a seven, when I go to a counselor to talk through childhood trauma the counselor has never told me, "That wasn't real" or, "That really did not hurt you."

The purpose of the doctor's or counselor's accepting posture is to find the pain and help the patient get to a place of health and healing. The best way to be of service to someone is to see things from their vantage point, to understand their pain and their experience, and to accept that it is different from your own.

We see this in Jesus' example here on earth. Jesus was never blind, yet He healed a blind man. He never had leprosy, but He healed the lepers. Jesus made Himself a humble servant to those who experienced things He never would, and He was harsher (rightfully so) on those who appeared to have more in common with Him. Jesus never sinned, yet He came down, saw our condition, and died for us anyway.

Why?

Because Jesus knew the importance of experiencing what we are experiencing.

Now is the time for us to decide: Are we going to be the partner in the room or are we going to follow the path of the generations before us and sit in a separated area hoping that all goes well?

When it comes to having conversations, are we going to empathize with what the other person is experiencing?

I know I have made my choice, and I think you have too. Your decision to read this book shows that you want to be in the room and you want to sit at the family table, but you just aren't sure how. I do not profess to be the expert on racial reconciliation, just as Irene's Lamaze teacher was not a medical doctor. But I have experienced a lot of pain and a lot of pressure, moments that were so intense I thought I would be ripped apart. I have experienced things so powerful that it drove me to become a student of those experiences so I could help others. Together we will learn how to read the room, listen to the doctor, hold the patient, and remind them to breathe.

A willingness to experience life through the eyes of another person is one of the most powerful ways to come together and have meaningful conversations. When we are seeking to understand their experiences, our right words can build bridges over even the biggest chasms.

That's when your words will begin to have power.

When those kids were posting mean words about Jaden, he could've picked his team and jumped to the other side of the chasm. But instead he used his words to bridge the gap. Jaden reached out to the young man who'd wronged him and let him know that he was ready to step into this experience with him and find a way to move forward.

Jaden did not deny who he was: a young Black man attending that school. And the words the other kids said hurt. But even in that he extended forgiveness and offered himself to be of service.

Jaden is in on it.

He showed more restraint and godly character in that moment than I probably would have at his age. I'm proud and humbled to be his dad. That moment when we watched our boys work it out was sacred; it changed the atmosphere in the room. When our teenage sons shared their responses to this dark moment, there was unity in the room.

Their action, their "being in on it," caused us parents to cry, and it opened up a great conversation and moved us from friends to family. This is how to be in on it. This is how to keep your bearings in difficult moments in life and offer yourself as a service. This is how to be a bridge over division into unity and reconciliation. If our kids can be in on it, then we must be in on it too.

Is there someone God is placing on your heart as you read this section? Someone you feel like God is calling you to love? What is one way you can use your words to step into their world and experience life from their point of view? What is one way you can reach out to them today and begin to bridge the chasm between you?

4. Engage with People

Initiating conversations with a diverse group of people is not comfortable. And because of that, it can be really easy to give up on the fight and let comfort win. The fourth thing we must do is resolve to never settle and never stop fighting to engage in healthy dialogue with people.

Engaging with people on the other side of our lines is not easy. If it were, I wouldn't need to write this book. There are going to be times when you want to give up, let comfort win, and stay in your own home with your own in-group. But in those moments you have to remember that we cannot settle and we cannot stop.

We must combat comfort by committing to engage with people!

I don't know about you, but I'm not a big fan of crowds. A bunch of bodies packed into one place is not my idea of a good time. I like to be at home on my couch, play with my dogs, or go out to the golf course. My favorite sport is one where there are not a lot of people but a lot of wide-open spaces.

I wonder which you would choose. What is your preferred style of comfort? It is important to recognize that and discern when it's time to be comfortable and when it is not. My comfort is my home, my couch, my dogs. My comfort is playing golf with a friend or two. That's what makes me feel comfortable, but it is not what I am called to.

I am called to engage with people.

If I lived to be comfortable, I would not choose ministry. I may not even choose leadership. Having comfort at home is

LOVE OUTSIDE THE LINES

not a sin, but unchecked it can lead me into a place of apathy and isolation. If something as innocent and necessary as being comfortable in my home can cause me to forsake relationships or even obedience to ministry opportunities that God calls me to if left unchecked, then we all need to be careful what we consider comforting. If you are only engaging with people who don't look like you because you have to for work, but you are not comfortable spending time with them when you don't have to, you have to check that. You have to ask yourself why.

This is why Paul worked hard to be a servant to all people. He safeguarded his heart by intentionally entering people's lives, seeing things from their point of view. He had lived a life of religion previously, where things were black and white, conform or die. After he had an encounter with Jesus it changed his appetite—he had to be actively involved with this kingdom that Jesus spoke about.

Paul went from persecuting the people who didn't think like he did, to loving and giving up everything to find ways to engage with those people.

If you want to have life-giving and life-changing conversations with people, you have to be willing to say no to comfort. You have to be willing to get out and engage with them!

RIP THE ROOF OFF

All of this reminds me of one of my favorite stories in the Gospels. It's about a man who was paralyzed but had four friends who were willing to go to tremendous lengths to get him to Jesus. The story is worth reading together:

> When Jesus returned to Capernaum several days later, the news spread quickly that he was back home. Soon the house where he was staying was so packed with visitors that there was no more room, even outside the door. While he was preaching God's word to them, four men arrived carrying a paralyzed man on a mat. They couldn't bring him to Jesus because of the crowd, so they dug a hole through the roof above his head. Then they lowered the man on his mat, right down in front of Jesus. Seeing their faith, Jesus said to the paralyzed man, "My child, your sins are forgiven." (Mark 2:1–5 NLT)

The news spread. It was trending. Jesus broke the internet. He was home and healing people. Folks came from everywhere to crowd the house He was in: the religious, the nonreligious, the meticulous moralists, the loose-living immoralists, the defeated, the demoralized, everybody (1 Corinthians 9:20–22 MSG)! The house was packed.

It's interesting to me that although Jesus had caused the house to be full, it wasn't full of Jesus. My question is, were the people's hearts full of Jesus? As I read Mark 2, I wonder, was anyone concerned about the paralyzed man? Were people making room for him? Were they there to just receive the message from Jesus or to live out the mission from Jesus?

Jesus probably would've been a lot more comfortable in an empty house, spending the afternoon with His close friends, but

He understood the importance of having conversations with a wide and diverse group of people, even people who were far from God. He opened up the home He was in to anybody and everybody who wanted to join.

The house was packed, so it seems as if it was easier to see Jesus than to follow Him. Everyone needed Jesus, but this paralyzed man needed Him the most. He couldn't move; he couldn't crawl to touch the hem of His garment; he couldn't climb a tree to see Jesus above the crowds; he wasn't getting his own water, so there was no well to have a meetup. He needed Jesus. But he couldn't get to Jesus.

There might as well have been a sign that said "No Paralyzed People." There was no ramp for a wheelchair entrance, no special seating set aside. Everyone crammed the house to get what they needed. There may have been some who had pity as they walked past him on their way to "church" that night. There might even have been some people who told him that they would pray for him when they got there, or that if given the chance they would tell Jesus about him. I'm sure there were some people with good intentions, but many times good intentions will lead us astray.

Good intentions need action. In order to make an impact, good intentions require intentionality, thoughtful response, and effort.

Today in our national and personal conversations about race, people are paralyzed. People are paralyzed in fear, worried they are going to say or do the wrong thing. People are paralyzed in doubt, wondering if things will ever get better. There is a lack of trust on both sides, and it is keeping so many people paralyzed and unable to move across the line of division.

That means it's our job to go get them. It's our job to move beyond our lines and pick up people who can't move. It's our job to be like these four friends, who went to the man on his mat and picked him up when he couldn't move.

The four friends are my favorite characters in this story. I picture them hanging out that afternoon in their in-group, talking shop, and enjoying the day. But when they heard Jesus was in town, they realized they had a chance to find the healing their friend was desperate for. But getting to Jesus was going to require leaving their homes, breaking through barriers, and carrying their love across a line—or through a roof. So they lifted him up to the roof, ripped a hole in it, and lowered him down to Jesus.

These four guys changed the front door to the church. They couldn't get him in the front way, so they ripped the roof off. They lifted off the limit of what could be, and they lowered the man to the feet of Jesus.

That is the kind of action it takes to initiate conversations with people we typically wouldn't talk to.

That is the kind of action it takes to build bridges with people outside our in-groups.

That is the kind of action the apostle Paul was talking about when he called us to be in on it.

These four guys empathized with the paralyzed man so much that they decided to do whatever needed to be done to carry this man to Jesus.

The issue of racism is heavy. The issue of division is heavy.

And carrying people who have fallen or given up is heavy. But it's what we are called to do.

Here's what I love about this story. Scripture says, "When Jesus saw their faith" (Mark 2:5 NKJV). Whose faith? This moment messes with my theology a little bit, but it wasn't just the paralyzed man's faith; it was the whole crew's.

Did you know our faith can lead people to the feet of Jesus? For as long as we are willing and committed to carrying people to Him, there is still hope for healing.

This whole story was about proximity. I think it's cool that these four friends who could've been unified by their abilities had a friend with a disability. The paralyzed man didn't have proximity to Jesus, but his proximity to these four people helped him get proximity to Jesus.

Because of Jesus, we get forgiveness for our sins, but so much of the healing happens in the context of relationship. That's why the Bible says, "Therefore confess your sins to each other and pray for each other so that you may be healed" (James 5:16).

Sometimes church people think we can just confess our sins to God and everything is good. But the Bible tells us to also talk to one another about our racist thoughts or our harmful stereotypes.

This is why we have too many people walking around forgiven but not healed. The truth is, they still don't like certain people, so they aren't willing to enter into conversation with them and be honest about the sins in their hearts.

God forgives.

But think about all the healing we are missing out on because we are too proud to confess our sins to one another. Imagine what would've happened if my pastor friend and his family had said, "God forgives us. That's all that matters." Thank God they didn't do that; in fact, they did the opposite of that. They came right over and apologized, and that is what led to all the healing, trust, and intimacy between us.

Today the thought of having conversations with people of different ethnicities may be really uncomfortable. You may wish you could just stay in the comfort of your own home, but if we want to carry our love outside the lines, then we have to be willing to rip the roof off.

I have a good friend named Shawn Johnson who pastors Red Rocks Church in Denver, Colorado. Shawn's White. We met through ministry, and he has invited me to preach at his church multiple times and it has allowed us to build a relationship. It gave us an opportunity to discuss realities we both faced that were different. Over the last few years, we have had several conversations that have been painful but productive.

One day I shared with him the conversation I had with my son when he got his driver's license: "Don't wear your do-rag, keep your music down, and when you are pulled over put your hands at ten and two."

With tears in his eyes, he looked at me and simply replied, "I am privileged not to need to have that conversation with my sons."

This conversation brought a six-foot-three Black man and a five-foot-eight White guy from Denver who pastors an all-White church into a brotherhood. Since that time we have had many hard conversations. We refuse to let comfort keep us apart. Instead we are committed to stepping in and engaging in each other's worlds. We may not vote the same, we may not see the same, but we are both fighting for the same thing: making disciples of all people.

You can't do that from the comfort of your couch, and you can't do that from the comfort of your pew. You are going to have to get up and go. You are going to have to be willing to carry one another's hurts. You are going to have to enter into people's worlds, empathize with them, experience what they experience, and engage in their lives. And you are going to have to be willing to not just touch a person of another color but hold their hand and walk together!

This is our job.

It is not the government's job; it is not the "other race's" job; it's not the next generation's job. It is our job, the body of Christ—those of us who claim to follow Jesus—to be in on it and lead one another into reconciliation and unity, to bring the kingdom of God here on earth!

THE POWER OF CONVERSATION

The beauty of this Bible story about the man on his mat is that the four men did not heal their friend. Their love, compassion, commitment, and conversations brought him to a place of healing with Jesus. They were not the ones who caused him to be paralyzed, but they were used in his healing.

That pastor who hiked up that mountain in Wyoming and cried with me about an event two decades earlier that he had nothing to do with helped me heal. He may have never used the N-word in his entire life. He did not inflict the wound in my heart, but he was willing to enter into the conversation, which may have made this even more healing for me. His kind words, his humility, his apologizing for something he didn't do, ripped off a roof that brought me to a place of awareness of God's beautiful grace and forgiveness in this area of my life.

That's the power of conversation.

The pressure is not on us to heal, but the assignment on us is to love. The call is to commit to carrying on the conversation one day at a time. The call is to commit to community with people who are outside our lines. The purpose is for us to be in unity, to live lives on earth as it is in heaven. We do this through creating relationships, putting ourselves in places that we wouldn't normally be, and having critical conversations that are rooted in love and humility. We do this through listening and empathizing with one another. As we do, Jesus heals us and continues to draw us closer to Him and one another.

This is the goal: unity. Unified with Christ and in Christ. This is the kingdom of God brought to earth as it is in heaven. If our goal is to make a point, we will never reach the goal of making a difference. We have to check our desire to make a point so that we can make a difference.

Are you ready to keep your eyes open for opportunities to enter into conversations? Are you ready to forgive and let go of any bitterness so your heart can be ready for those conversations? Are you ready to use your words to help bridge some barriers that stand between you and someone else? Are you ready to put all the pieces of this book together and take any step necessary to have some conversations with people who don't look like you?

I think it's time for us to put our mouths where the mission of Jesus is. Our mouths get us in trouble a lot, but if our words are aligned with the mission of Jesus, then we can use words that heal people instead of hurting them.

It's time for the body of Christ to be a part of the solution instead of the pollution.

Are you ready to be in on it?

——————————— HEART CHECK ———————————

- When is the last time you had a fruitful conversation with someone who didn't look like you? How did the conversation begin?
- How have you allowed comfort to hinder you from pursuing relationships with diverse people?
- As you notice any unforgiveness in your heart, where did it come from and how is it keeping you from having conversations?
- Who is one person you can reach out to today who will force you to get outside your comfort zone?

By the help of the Holy Spirit, allow me to authentically be who You created me to be and audaciously love those who are uniquely different from me. Lead me down a personal road of reconciliation that equips me to change things rather than complaining or being complacent about what needs to be changed. As I get ready to step into fruitful conversations with those who are different from me, anoint me to be a picture of grace and a representation of Your love in action.

NINE

THE GAME PLAN

This isn't a wish, this isn't just a
prayer, it's a mandate.

It was 1983, and I was nine years old playing on a local basketball team. At the time we were semi-undefeated; we only had two losses. Those losses were to the same team, all because they had a secret weapon. This secret weapon was a kid who was a foot taller and much stronger than any person on our team.

In my nine-year-old eyes, that foot may as well have been three feet. He was Michael Jordan and LeBron James wrapped up in one person. This kid was amazing, and my team and I were intimidated to say the least. We were in the playoffs and about to go out and play. Right before the whistle blew, my dad, the coach, pulled us together for some final words. To this day I have not forgotten what he said.

Bending down to look us in the eyes, he said, "Look, I know that y'all are scared and that kid is strong, but he isn't stronger than all of us together. I have a plan. This is what I want us to do: we are going to play as a team; we are going to move the ball around; we are not going to waste any opportunities; and most importantly, no matter how far down we are, we are never going to give up."

In the face of almost certain failure, my father came up with a four-part plan for success.

And that is exactly what we did. We went out there and played as a team, we kept moving the ball around, we didn't waste any opportunities, and we did not give up.

We were in the final quarter and tied. We had managed to stick with them that long, but to win the game, we needed one more basket. We took a time-out and my father looked up and down the bench at the team, scheming our next move. I started to hyperventilate at the thought of him picking me. I had sweat running down my face, and all of a sudden, my mother was at my side with a paper bag to breathe into. I still don't know where she got that bag from or how she got down those bleachers so fast to me, but she was there, and my father looked at me.

"Jimmy, you're up."

He picked me to make that final shot that would break the tie. I still can't believe and don't understand why he picked me. And I still don't understand how my mom was ready to support me so quickly.

You and I are warring against an opponent who's not some five-foot nine-year-old who is a beast on the basketball court. We are playing against a big stronghold that has been around since the fall.

We are playing against several generations of racism.

We are playing against several generations of line drawing.

We are playing against several generations of name calling.

We are playing against several generations of deeply embedded beliefs.

And yet, I'm convinced my father's game plan will work for us today.

DEFINING OUR WIN

In John 10:10 Jesus said that the Enemy comes to steal, kill, and destroy. We see him killing relationships, stealing hope, and destroying unity daily. As tensions rise and we get closer and closer to Jesus returning, the stakes are being raised. Jesus crossed over the line of heaven to bring us abundant life but also to give us the game plan.

Remember in chapter 7 when we read the story about Peter's proximity to Jesus? Jesus asked him who he thought He was, and because Peter had been near Jesus for a long time, he was able to answer correctly. Well, right after that moment, Jesus said something stunning to Peter: "Blessed are you, Simon son of Jonah, for this was not revealed to you by flesh and blood, but by my Father in heaven. And I tell you that you are Peter, and on this rock I will build my church, and the gates of Hades will not overcome it" (Matthew 16:17–18).

The Greek word for "church" is *ekklesia*, and this is the first time it's used in the Bible. Jesus used that word to give us the game plan. He used it to describe what He was building the revelation of who He was on.

The word *ekklesia* means "an assembly of people."[1] It is the people that make an *ekklesia*, not a foundational structure. When Jesus said that He was building His *ekklesia*, He made it everyone's duty, not just the priest and the preacher but the banker, the mail carrier, the lawyer, the cashier, the butcher, the baker, the candlestick maker—everybody. It is our duty to carry the message of who Jesus is, the Son of the living God, to all people.

All throughout the Gospels, Jesus crossed over lines and taught His disciples how to invite everyone to follow Him. And then, right before He ascended into heaven, He gave all of them (and all of us) a really important job. He said, "Therefore go and make disciples of all nations" (Matthew 28:19).

We call this the Great Commission, and it's the win for the *ekklesia*.

Fulfilling the Great Commission is the north star for the church. Our job is not to make duplicates of ourselves; it's to make disciples of Jesus. Because need has no color, we all have a need for healing, a need for significance. Divorce has no color. Fear has no hair texture. Anxiety and grief have no class distinction. Tears and pain have no language barrier. Our need for Jesus to redeem and fix these things unites us; our need for a savior was God's game plan. The thing that divides us—sin—is the same thing that unites us. If we aren't united in this commitment to make disciples of Jesus everywhere we go like Jesus did, we are not being the church and we will lose the battle of souls for eternity.

Crossing every border and boundary to successfully complete the mission and fulfill the Great Commission is how we win the game.

So my final question is, "How are we going to do that?" Like my basketball team, we are facing tremendous odds, which means we need a game plan. What's our game plan for fulfilling the Great Commission?

Completing the Great Commission is an ongoing process, but our team is being called to move the ball down the court. We have to keep going, and the best way to do that is to follow the same game plan my father gave us.

Play as a team.

Move the ball.

Don't waste any opportunities.

Never give up.

PLAY AS A TEAM

My father served in the army and fought in the Vietnam War.

During the day, as the men would be in the actual gunfight, American soldiers of all colors were fighting for the same thing. He told me there was no name-calling, division, or status in the foxhole. They were one unit, fighting against the same enemy.

Bullets were flying at them all day long, and it did not matter who was standing next to you or what color they were. During the fight, they played as a team.

But that was a stark difference to what it looked like when they were not fighting in combat. At night, after staying alive through another day, they would head to the bar and party.

As soon as they got to the bar, different in-groups would form. The team that was united all day would become divided and go drink at the bar with everyone clustered together in their own groups with their own kind.

My dad says he'll never forget the night they found out that Martin Luther King Jr. had been assassinated. During the day he had fought hand in hand with a White guy and actually saved his life. In the foxhole they were a team. But that night the same White guy walked over to my dad's all-Black group, laughed, and said, "We killed your leader."

When we are not fighting for the same thing, we are divided. When we are not fighting the same enemy, we start to look at one another as enemies.

We have to be the same people fighting in the foxhole as we are partying with our friends. In Vietnam there was unity in the foxhole but division at the bar. There was unity when things were life or death, but in a more relaxed setting comrades became strangers.

What are we doing in the church?

What are we doing as believers?

Is race only important to you because it is a hot topic right now, or are you committed to bringing change after the cameras stop rolling? We have to play as a team on and off the court, in the trenches and in our recreational time. If playing together as a team is important for a basketball game, if unity is so vital to win a war on earth, how much more vital is it for us to be unified in the war for our souls that goes on every single day? The Enemy doesn't take breaks. We may think that we have "off time" to kick back with friends, but we don't clock in and clock out when loving people to life. We have to play as a team. And there are no time-outs.

We are on the same team when we are fighting the same enemy. And when we are fighting for the same thing, there is nothing we cannot overcome. Jesus said of His church, "The gates of hell shall not prevail against it" (Matthew 16:18 ESV). Are we working together? Think about the experience my dad had in the foxhole. When soldiers were fighting for the same thing, they were the same. When they weren't fighting for the same thing, they were separated and became enemies. They defaulted to the cultural norms of segregation and prejudice. If we do not play as a team by keeping Jesus first, keeping the kingdom culture first, we will be divided.

As the clock was counting down, sticking with my dad's game plan became all the more vital. We had to keep playing as a team.

MOVE THE BALL

On a basketball team we must trust one another enough that if I pass you the ball, you are going to be willing to pass, take the shot, or do whatever is needed for us to keep that ball moving to and into the basket. It is the reason why we got on the court in the first place. So when the ball is passed to us, we have to be willing to take the shot.

As I said before, when it came down to the final moments, when a shot needed to be taken, my father looked up and down that bench and my response was to start hyperventilating. In my nine-year-old mind this game was everything. And the risk of missing—of letting my team down, letting myself down, letting the fans rooting for us down, and worst of all letting my father down—was too much to bear. Not only did I not want to do it, but my body physically did not want to do it.

What if I messed up?

I had spent so much time practicing and playing the game that taking the shot in the big moment was not new to me, but the stakes were so much higher. I really did not want to take the chance.

Isn't it crazy that it was so much easier for me to believe that I would fail at something I had worked hard at than to believe that I would be successful? Fear can do that to you. Fear can paralyze you in ways that are completely illogical. That was not my first time on the court. I had taken that shot hundreds of times, but fear made me feel like I had never played at all.

I bet you have been talking and having conversations since you were a toddler. I'm sure your parents rejoiced over your first words. If you are a pastor or a communicator like me, you live in words all day long. And yet when it comes to discussing race, isn't it crazy that fear of rejection will paralyze you in ways that leave you with no words when it is time to talk about race with someone of a different race?

Every one of us has been communicating, in some way, for our entire lives. But when it really counts, when the game is on the line, we can hyperventilate, freeze, and become paralyzed to take a shot at the conversation. When it comes to conversations about race, we are afraid to offend, afraid to say the wrong thing, afraid to appear ignorant, or worst of all, afraid to be called a racist.

But we must keep the ball moving, and we do that by building relationships and having conversations about the things that affect us deeply. We keep the ball moving by seeking more understanding. We must let go of the fear that we are going to lose the ball or miss the shot. We will miss the shot 100 percent of the time if we aren't willing to take it.

Whether it is on the basketball court or in life, a lack of communication is still communication. Silence still speaks, and it is a poor communicator as it gets misconstrued often. We have to be willing to work at relationships with people who are not the same as we are, and as we build those relationships, we ask questions. We ask about each other's experiences without making it about ourselves. We pray for the things that concern the other person even if we do not understand it fully. And when we are out together, we are aware of moments when our friends and loved ones may be treated differently by others.

I remember my dad coaching us the Saturday before that game. He was telling the team everybody can take the shot. Everyone had to realize their importance and value to the team in order to be able to take the shot. We can't just depend on certain players; we can't just depend on certain churches, certain leaders, or even certain laws to win the game for us. We have to move the ball and all be ready to take the shot.

So what will you do when you have the ball in your hands? If world change is up to you, does our team have a chance to win with the ball in your hands?

DON'T WASTE ANY OPPORTUNITIES

I find myself in game-changing moments more and more as I walk in obedience to carry love outside the lines.

Irene and I were once invited to share at the annual Celebrate Recovery Summit. This ministry is so important to our family as we are openly walking in recovery from our own addictions. At the time of this writing my wife is celebrating six and a half years of sobriety from an alcohol addiction, and God is using her to help others walk in their freedom. Walking into that conference, we looked around; it was predominately white and held in the South. It could have made us feel a little uncomfortable, but we have dealt with our uneasiness in situations where we are the minority.

We were not there to address anything about diversity or uprooting the roots of racism. We were there to talk recovery, to talk freedom from addictions, and God blessed this time with a powerful demonstration of His healing. People were running to the altar to receive healing and freedom. It was a beautiful time, and we were grateful to be a part of it. After the session ended, I went backstage and was overwhelmed at what God had just done. I thought He was finished; I had no idea what was about to happen next.

Suddenly a White woman was pushing past security, running to find me. She was running at me with purpose and passion. She had a look on her face like she couldn't believe what had just happened. It was a mix of wonder, fear, shame, and guilt.

She was crying as she said to me, "I don't know what I'm supposed to say, but I am a racist. As soon as you got up to speak, I wanted to walk out, and then the Holy Spirit had me stay. I heard your recovery story and God did something to my heart as I listened. I have said horrible things to Black people and done horrible things to Black people, and I want to change. I don't know what to say or do, all I know is I'm convicted and I want to try to go back and undo my wrongs and be a part of healing those I hurt."

I was blown away.

"I want you to know," I assured her, "that God has forgiven you and so do I."

When I asked if I could hug her, she admitted that she had never hugged a Black person before, but she agreed. I hugged and prayed for her, and her look of fear went away. Irene and I didn't go to the conference to talk about racism. We didn't allow ourselves to be uncomfortable because we weren't around people who looked like us. We simply went to be with people and share the story that God had given us.

We were available, and He did the rest. There is power in simply walking in obedience to God and bearing His fruit. The Holy Spirit truly does the heavy lifting. He is the one who brings unity, He is the healer, and He is the source.

What if I had decided not to go to the summit? What if I had decided that because the largest topic God has put on my heart has been racial reconciliation, I would only go to places that were asking me to speak on that topic?

Irene and I have walked into so many places where we were either the only or one of very few Black people present and have made beautiful friendships with people who don't normally hang around Black people. What if we didn't go? With God nothing is lost, and just because an invitation does not come in the package you expect does not mean it is a waste of time. Look around you—there is no lack of opportunities; we just need to make sure we are open to them. We don't even have to look for them.

I did not look for that opportunity to minister to that lady. I went into a place I was invited to. I was completely myself, and I did not have to force anything; I just had to be open when the opportunity came. This can be the same for you. Are there people you pass by daily, possibly colleagues at work, that you do not have any exchanges with other than email or professional questions?

These are opportunities. Ask people about themselves. Most people *love* to talk about themselves and their experiences.

Never miss an opportunity!

NEVER GIVE UP

When it comes to basketball, Michael Jordan is often considered the GOAT (greatest of all time). But my favorite quote from Jordan has more to do with his failures:

I've missed more than nine thousand shots in my career. I've lost almost three hundred games. Twenty-six times I've been trusted to take the game-winning shot and missed. I've failed over and over and over again in my life. And that is why I succeed.[2]

What if Michael Jordan had decided to give up the first time he missed a shot or had a turnover? A turnover is when you aim to pass the ball to your teammate, but your opponent intercepts it instead. Turnovers happen in every game at some point and are pretty critical. Games have been lost due to turnovers, and games have been won due to turnovers; it just depends on whose team you are on.

But do you know the worst thing that could happen with a turnover? If the team that had the ball gave up because they lost possession. Turnovers happen. Basketball players train and develop strategy on how to get that ball back into their hands or in the hands of their teammates.

In the same way, we can drop the ball when we become offended by the words and behaviors of others. We could be doing our best, moving the ball, having conversations, and building relationships, and before we know it, something we say or do might offend the person we have been building a relationship with.

That's a relational turnover that can make us want to give up.

When you get angry and say something you wish you could take back to a coworker, that's a turnover.

When you snap at someone you were trying to build a friendship with, that's a turnover.

When you turn the ball over, you give it back to the Enemy and you have to start playing some defense. And where you once may have felt confident and were having fun, you now feel tense and maybe even a little scared. You may feel like you will never be able to get back into a place where your team—or the kingdom—is winning.

Don't give up.

God has a strategy, and it is called forgiveness and reconciliation. Keep communicating, keep trying to understand, keep loving, keep having empathy. Just keep going. Never, ever, ever give up. The moment you give up is when the Enemy will continue to use that control to take over everything the team has worked so hard for. We must be persistent to keep playing as a team and win this war over our unity in Jesus.

About eight years ago I was in a room with a bunch of pastors I was not familiar with and we were talking. One guy who struck up a conversation with me was a pastor in Mississippi, and I am embarrassed to say that I prejudged him. By the nature of his geography, by the color of his skin, by the drawl of his voice, I had already decided in my mind that not only did he probably not want to talk to me, but when he heard what the driving message of my heart was he certainly was not going to be interested. I'd experienced it before. Not with him, but with others. And unfortunately our hearts have muscle memory.

So imagine my surprise when he turned to me and said, "You are Jimmy Rollins, aren't you? I'm glad to meet you. I pastor a church in Mississippi, and I really want to help my congregation become more diverse. I have heard some of your messages on this topic and it has helped me some."

I couldn't have been more surprised. So I listened as he told me about his efforts to help his church—a congregation that has gathered in a building for generations—become more diverse. This pastor had his heart set on building a diverse church filled with the different kinds of people that made up the community. For years he had preached the messages, invited guests in, tried to diversify his staff, and tried to reach out to different parts of his community. After years of trying everything he could with no real results, his frustration gave way to resignation. One afternoon during a quiet part of the week at the church, there was a knock at the door.

On the other side stood an elderly Black lady who asked him if he was the pastor and would walk with her to see something. Being a gentleman, he was not going to deny a request from this senior citizen, and he followed as she took his hand and led him to a tree on the church's property.

She attended a different church but had heard about his desire to diversify, and she knew the perfect place to start.

"Slaves hung on this tree," she said. "If you want to diversify this church, you have to chop down this tree."

That moment of awareness hit him so profoundly. Here he was doing all that he could, and there was an inanimate object that was triggering and keeping people from the vision. With this newfound knowledge and a new sense of hope, he gathered the men of the church for a tree-cutting service. Many people were excited to come out with their chainsaws and chop the tree down. The whole church rallied around and celebrated each and every limb that came off until the tree came crashing down and only the stump was left. As he told me all of this, I got excited with him.

Then he said, "But we still aren't where we want to be yet."

To which I replied, "What did you do with the stump?"

He responded that they'd done nothing, puzzled at the question.

"But what is the use of cutting down the tree," I asked, "if you do not remove the stump? Go back and remove the stump and see what happens."

I went on to explain that the stump represents the root system. And the roots represent that there is still something beneath the surface that needs to be addressed. You can remove a tree, but if you are trying to build a new foundation, you have to remove the roots.

Conversations can cut things down, but our calling is to completely uproot negative stereotypes and remove anything that is causing us to draw lines against others.

I wonder if the reason we want to give up is because we still haven't removed the stump in our hearts. After I left Bible college, I cut down the tree, but I let the stump of bitterness remain in my heart for twenty years. And as much as I loved my family and was proud of where we had been, when I was in the Great Rift Valley, I had to come face-to-face with the stump of anger I had let sit in my heart.

While I was talking to that pastor from Mississippi, I realized what was going on. They had cut down the tree, but they hadn't removed the stump. And it was really hard for his congregation to find the motivation and the courage to move outside the lines when they had a giant stump inside the lines of the church.

What's the use of cutting down the tree if we aren't going to remove the stump? Because the truth is, the roots run deep.

Adam ate from the tree.

Jesus was crucified on the tree.

And slaves were hanged on the tree.

The roots of racism are real. The roots of division run deep. And if we want to heal, we need to get all the way down to the depths and remove the stump.

Don't let this just be a book about cutting down branches. Let these words motivate you to do the work to remove the stump. If we are going to love outside the lines, we are going to need to go below the surface and deal with the roots.

If the thought of loving outside the lines is still hard for you, don't give up. Keep digging down into the roots and working to remove the stump. If you keep trying to carry love outside the lines but aren't seeing any fruit, don't give up. And if you are growing weary of trying to bring unity to a divided world, don't give up. Remember the reason it is so difficult to carry love outside the lines is because there is a giant stump deeply rooted inside the lines of our nation and our world.

But don't give up.

Every time we attempt to love someone who doesn't look like us, talk to someone who doesn't speak like us, or understand someone who doesn't think like us, we are chipping away at the racist root system and playing our part to remove the stump.

If you've learned anything from this book, I hope it's that

God can remove your stump, remove your community's stump, and redeem your story.

So don't give up.

You've come so far; you can't give up now.

THE GAME PLAN IN ACTION

Here's one final, simple story that sums up our game plan to carry our love outside the lines.

I recently had a conversation with a new friend who is White. He and I have just begun our friendship and I appreciate our times together. We were going into a store to look at some appliances and electronic equipment and a saleswoman started a conversation with us. She was kind and friendly.

Suddenly she asked me out of nowhere, "So are you an athlete? What sport do you play?"

I could see my friend fidget at that moment and begin to look uncomfortable as I explained that I wasn't an athlete, just a regular guy coming in to check out some stuff.

As we got into the car and began to drive away, he said, "What she asked you, that really bothered me. Does that bother you?"

I was taken aback for a moment. I knew he was uncomfortable, but I didn't think that he would bring it up. And I'm very glad he did. This was one of those small moments we could've moved right past, but instead we decided to stop and have a conversation about it. My friend decided that since we are on one team, he would pass me the ball and learn from my experience.

I said, "Yeah, it bothers me, but I'm kind of used to it."

His response was that he didn't want me or anyone else for that matter to ever get used to that. He paused for a while, and I could tell he was really thinking about this, so I decided not to waste this opportunity.

I said to him, "There is a difference between intention and impact. I don't think she intended it to be a racist question, and she doesn't realize the impact of her ignorance."

Many times people say things out of not knowing any better, and we are expected to brush it off because that person wasn't aware. This person may not intend to be hurtful, but the impact of those words does hurt. The thought that I've been labeled hurts. Yeah, she may have been labeling me in a positive light because I could afford something, but what if I couldn't afford that thing? What would my label have been then? She didn't intend to judge, but there is an impact with that judgment.

Instead of responding or reacting, he kept passing me the ball. He then asked me, "Do you think she is racist?"

I loved his willingness to listen and learn.

"No," I said. "I don't know her, but I'm sure she hasn't had proximity with Black people who are educated and successful outside of sports. If she had, she would not rely on stereotypes to try to identify with me."

Then he asked me, "Do you think it will ever change? Do you think this will change for our kids?"

"That all depends on the conversations you are willing to have, with your kids and with others," I said.

I began to share with him about what I've been working on

with this book and the things that God has shown me through the years.

He agreed and said, "I would have never been able to have this conversation with you had we not been friends."

It's friendship—the choosing to be unoffendable, the leaving nothing unsaid, and being committed to let nothing come between us—that is going to help us build bridges.

As the body of Christ, we are a team, and when we start playing and acting like it, we've got a shot at winning the game. We can fulfill the Great Commission by carrying God's love outside the lines and into all nations, but to do that we have to play as a team, move the ball around, stop wasting opportunities, and never give up.

Before we parted, he asked me, "Are you hopeful that this racial divide in our country will change?"

"I don't know," I told him. "*Hopeful* may not be the right word. This isn't a wish, this isn't just a prayer, it's a mandate. I don't know if it will ever change, but I am going to be faithful to my assignment and never give up."

I am going to be faithful one conversation at a time. I don't know if it will ever change, but I am going to die trying. I will remain faithful to this assignment, and I pray that God has stirred something in you, that you take hold of the assignment to love outside the lines and remain faithful, one person, one conversation at a time.

Things may not look hopeful, but we can't ever give up.

When my dad sent me back into the basketball game when

everything was on the line, I followed his orders. By that point a large crowd had gathered in the gymnasium. No one expected us to still be in the game, but we were. And everyone was watching to see if we had what it took to take down the best team in the league.

As I dribbled up the court, I could see the clock winding down.

10 . . .
9 . . .
8 . . .
7 . . .

The kid who was their star player, the one who had intimidated me before, could tell I was the one who was about to take the shot, so he ran up and met me at half court.

6 . . .
5 . . .
4 . . .

I made my move and found just enough space to throw up a prayer. I took the shot as my dad, my teammates, and the entire crowd held their breath and watched.

3 . . .
2 . . .
1 . . .

As the buzzer sounded, the ball went through the hoop. The crowd went crazy! Everyone stormed the court, and the next thing I knew I was being mauled by all my teammates.

My dad's plan worked. We won the game!

In the end, this is how we win. If we want to fulfill the Great Commission and carry God's love outside the lines to all people, not just some people, we are going to have to follow the same strategy. We must get in God's game plan where we play as a team, move the ball around, don't waste opportunities, and never give up!

──────── HEART CHECK ────────

- When you take an honest look at your heart, is there still a stump of bitterness there? Have you been trying to cut off the branches instead of removing the stump? If so, where did the stump come from and how can you start removing the roots?
- Where have you missed opportunities to love outside the lines recently? What could you have done differently? What will you do when you are given the opportunity again?
- How has fear paralyzed you in this area in the past? Are you willing to take the shot now? Specifically, what will that look like in your life?
- If you are honest, do you want to give up? What is one line, or big idea, from this book that you can carry with you to motivate you to keep going when you want to quit?

Dear Lord, make me an agent of change in the current culture of division in our world. Help me to carry the love and acceptance of Jesus over every line that is around me. As I follow You, bring me to opportunities that bridge the gap of unity and heal the rifts that keep us divided. I pray that You give me the tenacity to never give up despite what looks like insurmountable odds. I want to play as a team and win as a team, so would You bring the right people around me? And please give me the humility and the boldness to play as a team, move the ball around, seize every opportunity, and never give up!

NOTES

Chapter 1

1. Dictionary.com, s.v. "rift," accessed May 9, 2022, https://www
.dictionary.com/browse/rift.

2. "Father Abraham," written by Pierre Kartner, lyrics from
Cedarmont Kids, 1995, accessed June 17, 2022, https://open
.spotify.com/track/6RN9GQyatptNREQ86XnDFO
?si=x2rYR64wShKSSRRY_3hPtw.

Chapter 3

1. YourDictionary, s.v. "stronghold," accessed June 6, 2022,
https://www.yourdictionary.com/stronghold.

2. "Metanoia Meaning in Bible - New Testament Greek Lexicon -
King James Version," Bible Study Tools, accessed March 15, 2022,
https://www.biblestudytools.com/lexicons/greek/kjv/metanoia
.html.

Chapter 4

1. *Oxford Dictionary*, s.v. "dignity," accessed May 16, 2022, https://
www.lexico.com/en/definition/dignity.

2. "Eschatos Meaning in Bible - New Testament Greek Lexicon

- New American Standard," Bible Study Tools, accessed March 22, 2022, https://www.biblestudytools.com/lexicons /greek/nas/eschatos.html.

Chapter 6

1. C. H. Woolston, author, "Jesus Loves the Little Children," accessed June 19, 2022, https://hymnary.org/text /jesus_loves_the_little_children_all_the.
2. Martin Luther King Jr., *Strength to Love* (Boston: Beacon Press, 1963), 47.

Chapter 7

1. Martin Luther King Jr., Interview on *Meet the Press*, Washington, DC, April 17, 1960, http://okra.stanford.edu/transcription /document_images/Vol05Scans/17Apr1960 _InterviewonMeetthePress.pdf.

Chapter 9

1. "Ekklesia Meaning in Bible - New Testament Greek Lexicon - New American Standard," Bible Study Tools, accessed June 13, 2022, https://www.biblestudytools.com/lexicons/greek/nas /ekklesia.html.
2. Henry Blodget, "Check Out This Awesome Michael Jordan Quote About Success," *Business Insider*, November 3, 2011, https://www.businessinsider.com/michael-jordan -success-2011-11.

ACKNOWLEDGMENTS

Irene: Thank you for everything you do and for everything you are. Your belief in me is indescribable. I can't believe God loves me so much that He trusted me with someone like you. Your heart has endless capacity, your strength refuses to give up, and your eyes have always seen the best in me, even when I couldn't see it in myself. Thank you for being a picture of God's love in action. You are a real-life picture of God's grace and faithfulness.

Kayla, Jaden, and Maya: You all are my joy, my strength, and my greatest cheerleaders. Without your laughter, I would not know joy. And your encouragement is the fuel that gives me the confidence to continuously pursue the purposes of God for my life and our family. You all have had a front-row seat to my greatest struggles and my greatest successes, and I only hope that I continue to make you proud. I love each of you more than words can describe.

Mom and Dad: I would not be here without you both. Other than my wife, no one has believed in me more and encouraged me greater than both of you. The message of this book has been instilled in me by you since birth. Since I was a child, you have put me on a trajectory to always pursue God's purpose for my life. You have modeled marriage ministry and family to me in such an amazing way. You have both been an example of God's faithfulness and have shown me what it looks like to remain faithful no matter the season. Thank you for never compromising, never quitting, and always loving everybody. I pray that I continue to make you proud.

Tonya Dorsey: Since I can remember, I've looked up to you. You have lived with purpose, pursued excellence, and thrived in every environment you've been in. You have always been a source of encouragement for me and never allowed me to settle for anything less than God's best for my life. Thank you for always telling me there is greatness in me. This book is proof that I finally believe I can do it.

Kevyn Dodson: You have been a faithful friend since elementary school. We have fought together, cried together, and laughed together. But most importantly, we've always done life together. Since day one, your discipline, strength, tenacity, and grit have helped me endure the most difficult seasons of my life. Thank you for always being willing to get in my face and for pushing me to finish strong. Like we always say, "Can you believe all that

God has done and continues to do!" Let's keep impacting the kingdom together!

Dino and DeLynn Rizzo: I do not know where I would be without you both. Your love, support, and accountability are a huge part of the man I am today. From the moment we met, you have been consistent, gracious, and more than faithful friends. I cannot say thank you enough for helping me be all that God has called me to be and for always encouraging me to live out my call without making it about myself. There are few people like you in the world. Thank you for always representing the message of this book in my life. I love you both.

Andi Andrew: You are definitely my sister from another mister. Since day one, you have pushed me and have valued what God put inside me. Without your consistent encouragement and prophetic insight, this book would not be a reality. I'll never forget that day in the lobby of the Soho Grand when you told me to write this book. Thank you for all the connections, encouragement, and relationships that have turned this dream into a reality. And more than anything, thank you for always being a faithful friend.

W Publishing: Thank you for taking a risk on me and this book. Your encouragement and support have meant the world. Not only have you embraced the message of this book, but you have helped me interpret it in a way that I hope changes the world we

ACKNOWLEDGMENTS

live in. Thank you for not only embracing its message behind the scenes but for being willing to live it out practically and publicly.

And a huge thanks to all my brothers—you know who you are. Thank you for helping me live out the message of this book in the face of racism, stereotyping, and acts of injustice and apathy. Our FaceTimes, text messages, and phone calls have been purposeful and life-giving. You have encouraged me, held me accountable, and pushed me to write this book.

ABOUT THE AUTHOR

Jimmy is passionate about bridging the gap of division in our society and bringing solutions for greater unity to individuals, churches, and organizations. He is a champion for those who are outcasts, marginalized, and overlooked. With over two decades of full-time ministry experience, including ten years as a senior pastor, his wisdom and insight have become invaluable to many. Through his work in racial reconciliation, he has been able to teach and mediate conversations that bring forth awareness and healing across diverse sectors.

Jimmy and his wife, Irene, have been married and doing ministry together for twenty-three years. In 2020 they transitioned from leading i5 City, the church they launched, and founded Two = One, a marriage ministry helping couples discover their marriage equation—one of love, laughter, and longevity.

Jimmy continues to make a significant impact around the globe as an author, speaker, and marriage educator. Whether in a one-on-one conversation or communicating to thousands,

ABOUT THE AUTHOR

Jimmy's heart of compassion and infectious relational nature instantly connects him with diverse audiences. Through his vulnerable and transparent approach, Jimmy's heart for people to live to their fullest potential and pursue a greater purpose comes through in every facet of his life.

In his downtime, Jimmy enjoys playing golf, cooking, and spending time with Irene and their adult children, Kayla, Jaden, and Maya.